OKAVANGO
FROM THE AIR

OKAVANGO
FROM THE AIR

Photographs by Herman Potgieter

Text by Clive Walker

Foreword by Ian Khama

STRUIKHOF PUBLISHERS

ACKNOWLEDGEMENTS

Okavango From the Air has been a team effort not only by those who have helped us in the compilation of our material, but also by those who are dedicated to the preservation of the Okavango Delta. This book, therefore, is a tribute to all who share, love and hold dear the wild places that still remain on planet Earth.

Wild places are increasingly becoming islands in a sea of expanding humanity. We cannot prevent this process from continuing, but we can – and should – strive to preserve unique systems such as the Okavango for the benefit of everyone.

We are especially grateful to a number of people who made this book possible. June and Lloyd Wilmot and the staff at Lloyd's Camp, Savuti, afforded us their warm hospitality, advice and assistance. A special word of thanks to Lloyd and André Pelser of S.A. Airtours who so ably flew us, often in difficult conditions; to Major-General Ian Khama, who wrote the Foreword, and who has a deep love for the wildlife of Botswana; to our wives, Jackie and Conita, for their encouragement and patience; to Jonathan Gibson and the staff of Chobe Game Lodge, P.J. and Barney Bestelink, Sue and Ewan Masson, Gert Britz and Map Ives and the staff at Xugana Lodge, George Calef, Phil Nash, Anton Walker, Ursula Wilmot, Mike Main and Rozanne Savory; and to all those others, too numerous to mention, who helped to make our task easier.

Our thanks also to the directorate and staff of the Department of Civil Aviation for permission to carry out low-level flights, to the Department of Wildlife and National Parks for its valuable support, and to the Office of the President for permission to undertake this project in Botswana. Dennis da Silva of Beith is particularly thanked for superb processing of the film. Lastly, we should like to thank Dr. Thomas Tlou, Vice-Chancellor of the University of Botswana, and Alec Campbell, former Curator of the National Museum and Art Gallery, who have studied the human settlement of the Okavango Delta in detail, for information in this regard.

Struikhof Publishers (Pty) Ltd
An operating division of The Struik Group (Pty) Ltd
Struik House
Oswald Pirow Street
Foreshore
8001 Cape Town

Registration No. 71/09721/07

First published 1989

Copyright © 1989 in text Clive Walker
Copyright © 1989 in captions Clive Walker/Struikhof Publishers
Copyright © 1989 in photographs Herman Potgieter
Landsat images reproduced by kind permission
of the Satellite Applications Centre of the Council for
Scientific and Industrial Research (CSIR), Pretoria.

House editor: John Comrie-Greig
Design: Etienne van Duyker
Cover design: Abdul Amien

Typesetting by Diatype Setting cc, Cape Town
Reproduction by Unifoto (Pty) Ltd, Cape Town
Printed and bound in Singapore

ISBN 0 947458 04 2

Half-title page: Lloyd Wilmot's Cessna 175 flies over a group of Burchell's zebra on the Savuti Marsh in Chobe National Park.

Title page: A group of lechwe on a sandbar island in the clear waters of the Okavango River in the northern delta.

Foreword page: A hippopotamus wallows in a pool in the Savuti Channel not far from the Linyanti River.

Contents page: Even in the dry season the Savuti Marsh remains attractive to a wide variety of game animals. This bull giraffe stands alone in a yellow sea of winter-dry couch-grass or 'kweek'.

FOREWORD

It makes me very proud indeed to have in this country of mine one of the most spectacular natural features that exists in Africa, the Okavango – an area that can compete with the many breathtaking sites of world repute.

Those who have read books about the first explorers of the continent of Africa, and the type of riches they encountered in the form of abundant wildlife, flowing rivers, and colourful and vibrant birdlife, would certainly experience something of a taste of those days gone by, should they ever visit the Okavango. To a large extent it is still similar to what those first explorers must have seen. Obviously, over time, the area has slightly diminished due to changes brought about by man. However, reading and listening to stories about its character is no substitute for seeing it for yourself.

The author, Clive Walker, whom I know personally, has a very intimate knowledge of the area due to his tremendous involvement in nature conservation in the whole region. He has arranged several projects in Botswana in an attempt to assist the authorities in preserving the environment and those who depend solely upon it. Similarly in South Africa he has done, and continues to do, much in this regard. An example of this is the environmental education centre called Lapalala Wilderness School which he and his wife run in the Waterberg Mountains to educate young people about their natural heritage.

Finally, I do hope that most of you who read this book will have an opportunity to visit the Okavango. I have done so many times and each subsequent visit is like the first for me, a mirage of a paradise in the desert, which is actually there.

IAN KHAMA

CONTENTS

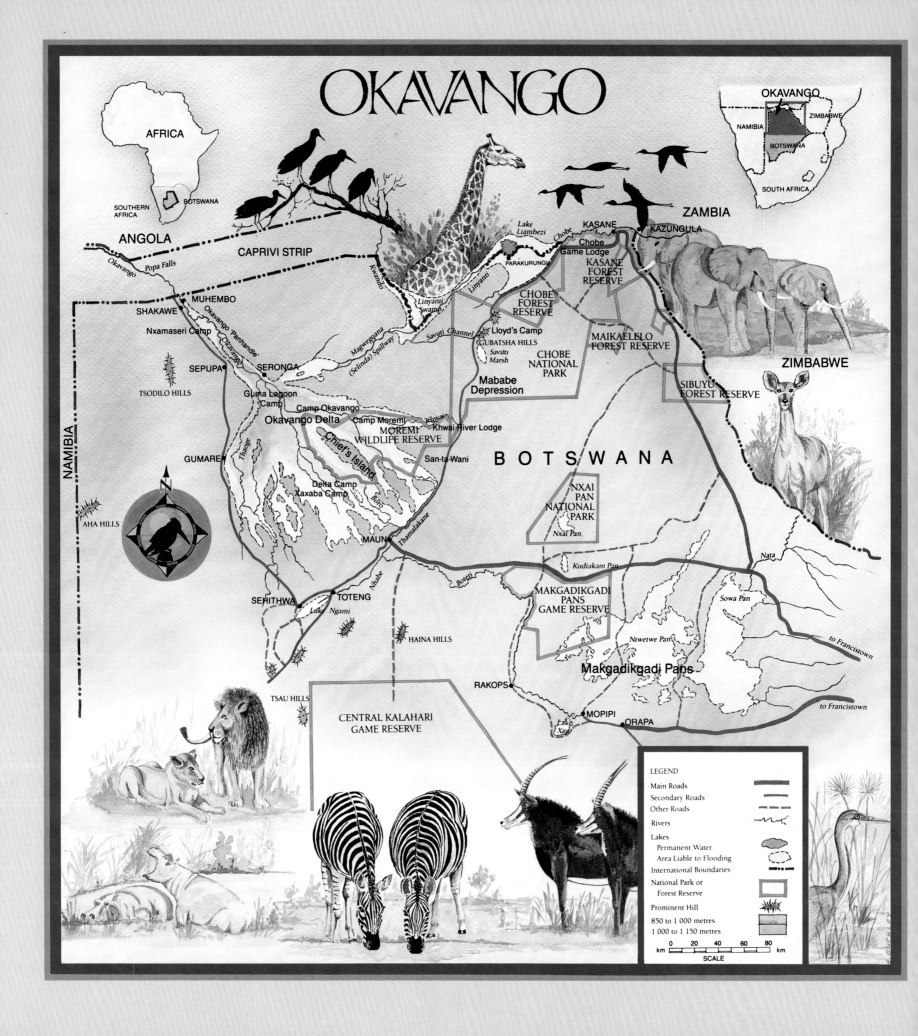

OKAVANGO

AFRICA

SOUTHERN AFRICA

BOTSWANA

OKAVANGO

NAMIBIA · ZIMBABWE · BOTSWANA · SOUTH AFRICA

ANGOLA

CAPRIVI STRIP

Okavango · Popa Falls

MUHEMBO

SHAKAWE

Nxamaseri Camp

Okavango 'Panhandle'

SEPUPA · SERONGA

TSODILO HILLS

Guma Lagoon Camp

Camp Okavango

Okavango Delta

Camp Moremi

GUMARE

Delta Camp
Xaxaba Camp

AHA HILLS

NAMIBIA

Thaoge

Boro

Chief's Island

MOREMI WILDLIFE RESERVE

Khwai River Lodge

San-ta-Wani

MAUN

Thamalakane

Nhabe

SEHITHWA · TOTENG

Lake Ngami

HAINA HILLS

TSAU HILLS

CENTRAL KALAHARI GAME RESERVE

Lake Liambezi · Chobe · KASANE · KAZUNGULA

ZAMBIA

PARAKURUNGU

Kwando

Linyanti swamp

Linyanti

Magweggana (Selinda) Spillway

Savuti Channel

Lloyd's Camp

GUBATSHA HILLS
Savuti Marsh

Mababe Depression

Chobe Game Lodge

KASANE FOREST RESERVE

CHOBE FOREST RESERVE

CHOBE NATIONAL PARK

MAIKAELELO FOREST RESERVE

SIBUYU FOREST RESERVE

ZIMBABWE

B O T S W A N A

NXAI PAN NATIONAL PARK

Nxai Pan

Kudiakam Pan

Boteti

Nata

MAKGADIKGADI PANS GAME RESERVE

Sowa Pan

Ntwetwe Pan

Makgadikgadi Pans

RAKOPS

to Francistown

Lake Xau

MOPIPI · ORAPA

to Francistown

LEGEND

Main Roads
Secondary Roads
Other Roads
Rivers
Lakes
  Permanent Water
  Area Liable to Flooding
International Boundaries
National Park or Forest Reserve
Prominent Hill
850 to 1 000 metres
1 000 to 1 150 metres

km 0 20 40 60 80 km
SCALE

INTRODUCTION

For decades people have been trying to unravel the secrets of the Okavango Delta – one of the true mysteries of creation. The delta is fed by the Okavango River which rises in the highlands of Angola, mushrooms into a wilderness of waterways in far northern Botswana, and dies in the Kalahari's Makgadikgadi Pans. Encompassing some 15 000 km² when it floods, the delta is said to have been covered at one time by a huge lake, far bigger than its present size.

Like many other people, I have been drawn to the Okavango by pure fascination – carried away by dreams of gliding along its waterways in a dugout canoe or *mokoro*. In 1978 I undertook my first journey to the delta, and since then the magic of the area has greatly influenced my own desire to know more about its origins, wildlife and people, and what may become of it.

Over the years, I have witnessed change and have listened to the pronouncements of what man has in store for the Okavango and the subsequent problems it faces. I have seen tourism increase in the region and have contributed to that development myself. The area serves not only to attract holidaymakers, artists, writers, scientists and conservationists, but also contributes to the national economy of Botswana by bringing in useful foreign currency and providing employment.

The Okavango Delta is a fragile region and while it has its fair share of threats, it is not this book's intention to dwell on them. Instead, we will take you on an awesome journey across this hauntingly beautiful land, looking at it as if through the eyes of an eagle. This aerial perspective is unique in a way, for it covers far more than just the Okavango Delta itself.

I first met Herman Potgieter, photographer of *Okavango From the Air*, in 1986 when I had been asked to give a series of illustrated lectures on wildlife conservation. The accompanying colour slides included aerial photographs of the Okavango Delta. Herman, a professional aerial photographer, was so captivated by what he saw that he suggested to me the possibility of doing an aerial overview of the delta. The idea interested me immediately.

Herman had never been to the Okavango, and therefore left it to me to make the preliminary arrangements for such a venture. Over the years, I had met many people working in northern Botswana and felt we were off to a good start.

The Okavango had previously been portrayed by others, but not in the way in which we intended approaching the subject – from the air. I also felt we had to take a holistic viewpoint and go beyond what is known as the Okavango itself. We decided to cover a far wider area than just the Okavango's 15 000 km² of wetland.

Our area incorporates Lake Ngami, at the southernmost corner of the delta, the Makgadikgadi salt pans, Nxai Pan, the Chobe National Park (which includes the Savuti Marsh), the Mababe Depression and Linyanti Swamp, and, finally, the Chobe River which flows into the Zambezi River and eventually over the mighty Victoria Falls.

In former times, Lake Ngami was a much larger body of water, fed by the Thaoge River which flows down the western side of the delta but no longer reaches the lake. The river starts as an offshoot of the Okavango River, at the southern end of the 'panhandle' (as the first 95 km of the Okavango River are described), but has in recent years suffered two natural blockages.

To the east, the Thamalakane River flows past the town of Maun, which is the focal point of the entire region and gateway to the Okavango. The Thamalakane runs past Maun in a south-westerly direction, and then splits into the Nhabe, which winds its way to Lake Ngami, and the longer Boteti, which carries the annual floodwaters towards the ancient Lake Makgadikgadi.

This 'fossil' lake once covered more than 60 000 km² and its remnants form the largest salt-pan system in the world. Makgadikgadi is the final destination of the run-off of water caused by the summer rains in Angola. This overflow is depleted en route by infiltration into the soil, by evaporation from open water surfaces as well as by absorption by plants and transpiration by their leaves.

The beautiful lake area, which has a seasonal abundance of wildlife, is made up of two large interconnecting pans, Sowa and Ntwetwe. Sowa Pan, in the east, is over 100 km long and 45 km wide, and Ntwetwe Pan in the west is even larger. The lowest and deepest parts of the fossil super-lake, the pans today are rarely covered by water. To the west lies the Makgadikgadi Pans Game Reserve and to the north-west the Nxai Pan National Park.

The Okavango Delta itself has at its centre Chief's Island, which lies in the Moremi Wildlife Reserve. Moremi stretches

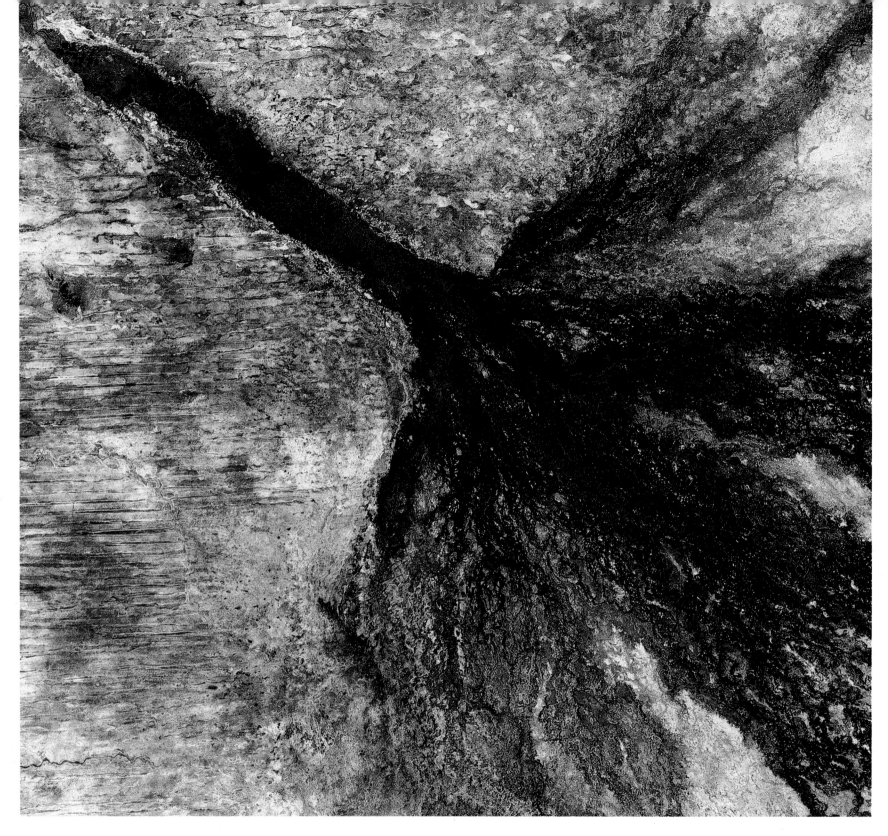

eastwards to the Khwai River, and then across the dry wood-land area adjacent to the Mababe Depression. North-east of the Okavango Delta, stretching from the eastern tip of the Moremi Reserve towards the confluence of the Chobe and Zambezi rivers, is the Chobe National Park, which includes the southern end of Savuti Marsh.

The park is home to some of the finest concentrations of big game left in Africa in its unspoilt state, and shelters the bulk of Botswana's elephant population. Habitats include rolling grasslands, sandy ridges with rocky outcrops, marsh-land, rivers, pans, extended woodlands and a 'fossil' lake bed – the Mababe Depression.

The Linyanti River forms the eastern boundary of the Linyanti Swamp – a vast wetland wilderness in the southern bulge of the Caprivi Strip and which extends marginally into Botswana. Further up, the Chobe River flows eastwards into the Zambezi.

This then is the area we have covered, and in this book I

will try to describe how its different parts are historically connected, the wildlife and wilderness on the fringes of these systems, the people who live there, and how they benefit from the increasing flow of tourism.

The Government of Botswana today grapples with increasing human development on the one hand – many of the people living in the western and southern region own cattle – and a rapidly expanding tourist industry on the other. And while the Government recognises it has a unique jewel in the wilderness area of northern Botswana, it realises it must address the needs of the ever-increasing human population and the effect these will have upon this greatest of African wetlands.

Thousands of people have been to the Okavango; some go seeking adventure; others to savour the atmosphere of wilderness and wildlife; still others visit Okavango to learn about the region's fauna and flora. No matter what the reason, all, I am sure, have left with indelible impressions of a

The Okavango Delta as seen from a satellite some 800 kilometres above the earth's surface.
Left: The north-western delta and 'panhandle'.
Above: The south-eastern delta showing the Thamalakane Fault, the eastward-flowing Boteti River, and the Mababe Depression.

truly unique wilderness area. The region has something for everyone, and it is not surprising that many fear the unhappy future it may face.

Herman and I flew from one end of Okavango to the other, in bumpy conditions and smooth. We evaded vultures and eagles and felt the cold dawn air rushing into our aircraft through the opening where the right-hand door had been removed to enable Herman to direct his camera. We saw fires burning in a dozen places, with huge columns of smoke rising into the clear blue sky; we witnessed buffaloes drive lions off a buffalo carcass and saw dust whipped up by the hoofs of hundreds of cattle rise up to our low-flying aircraft.

We saw huge crocodiles basking in the sun and hundreds

of pelicans swirling upwards in ever-increasing circles; we heard the roar of lions at dawn in the Savuti Channel as we prepared for take-off, and observed the slow, careful approach of a solitary roan antelope bull coming to water.

We were up in the air at dawn and down on the ground at sunset every day. When it became too hot, we would break off flying and land at base; we would eat first, then head out to the nearest water-hole by vehicle to spend hours watching game coming to quench their thirst. Here we would take more photographs and make copious notes. Back in the air again at about three in the afternoon, we would head for a new destination, witnessing again the never-ending panorama of changing light and colour in the bush.

Our pilots, André Pelser and Lloyd Wilmot, with whom I have worked and flown for years, know the area intimately, and their contribution was exceptional. They remained cheerful and uncomplaining in spite of being asked to circle certain areas again and again.

With expert flying, they took us to the right places at the right time and always ensured that we came home safely. They sat and helped with our advanced planning and contributed their expertise and knowledge. Their immense love for this whole region was an essential ingredient in the compilation of our material.

I began researching material for a book on the Okavango 10 years ago. Fortunately, the time taken to photograph the region was naturally far less; in fact, the material was mostly shot during 1987 and spread out over five trips.

We covered the four seasons with many hours of flying, moving from one area to the other swiftly. The sheer grandeur of the delta from the air is almost too much to absorb and eventually one has to come down to earth to be in touch with one's physical surroundings again.

While a good photographer can do justice to the region in pictures, one cannot really do justice to a subject of such magnitude in the space of a few thousand words. I have had to condense my thoughts into these brief chapters; forgive me, therefore, if we whisk you from one place to the other as if you were flying with us.

Shimmering light is reflected from the calm waters of the Okavango's numerous lagoons in the 'panhandle'. The Okavango River in the background winds sinuously over the plain before spilling out into the great fan of the delta.

Left above: Lloyd Wilmot's aircraft, a slow-flying Cessna 175, was admirably suited to the task of photographing the delta's wildlife from the air. Here he flies towards Maun across a dry sandveld region of Moremi Wildlife Reserve.

Left below: Heading south from Guma Lagoon, our Cessna 210 Centurion piloted by André Pelser passes over a herd of lechwe splashing through the shallows. Lechwe are rarely found more than a kilometre or two from the permanent water of floodplains or seasonal swamps.

Main picture: Three vintage De Havilland Tiger Moths in step-up echelon formation flying between Guma and Nxamaseri in the Okavango 'panhandle'. This flight was sponsored by a well-known international company and graphically illustrates the increasing popularity of the area as a tourist attraction – while at the same time gently reminding us that too much air traffic over the delta could adversely affect the peace and tranquillity of this splendid wilderness.

CHAPTER ONE

THE OKAVANGO ENVIRONMENT

The Okavango is an inland delta in the dry Kalahari sand-veld of northen Botswana, in the district of Ngamiland. Ngamiland stretches from the South West Africa/Namibian border in the west to the boundary of the Chobe National Park in the east. It is bounded in the north by western and eastern Caprivi.

The word Ngami comes from the Bayei word *Ncama*, which means 'floating mat of reeds'. This slight corruption came from the Batswana in the 18th Century and was later perpetuated by Europeans.

Within Ngamiland lies the great Okavango Delta, whose 15 000 km² cover about three per cent of Botswana's total land surface area of 582 000 km². According to Mike Main in his important work, *Kalahari, Life's Variety in Dune and Delta* (1987), the Okavango Delta is generally accepted as being at the most southern end of the massive continental fault known as the Great Rift Valley. This fault is thought to date from the mid-Miocene Epoch between 10 and 15 million years ago. The fault extends from the Dead Sea and Red Sea southwards through Kenya and the great lakes of East Africa; it then divides to include the Zambezi Valley and Zambia on one side, and Lake Malaŵi on the other.

The waters which form the delta originate in the Angolan Highlands to the north-west, less than 300 km from the Atlantic Ocean. The name Okavango is probably derived from the word Kubango, the name of a small community of people living near the border of South West Africa/Namibia, Caprivi and Angola. The word seems to have a Portuguese origin as it was not known historically to the earlier inhabitants of the Okavango Delta.

The well-known South African-born ecologist, Ken Tinley, in his report *An Ecological Reconnaissance of the Moremi Wildlife Reserve, Botswana*, states: 'No river in Ngamiland has a continuous name of its own. It is merely "the river" of such and such a place.' The origin of the name Okavango, therefore, must remain a mystery for the time being.

Dropping down from the highlands to the plains, the Okavango River flows south-eastwards, cutting its way for nearly 1 000 km through Angola and finally crossing the Caprivi Strip to empty into the delta. It enters Botswana at Muhembo where the inflow is some 11 thousand million m³ per annum, sufficient to cope with the water needs of England and Wales. It is at Muhembo that our story begins.

It has been estimated that the sand and sediment discharge of the Okavango River as it enters Botswana at Muhembo is between two and three million tons per annum. The sand settles out of the slow-moving water as the rising floods spread through the delta, often forming attractive miniature deltas where channels discharge into lagoons.

Xobega Lagoon, one of a spectacular series of oxbow lakes formed by the meanderings of the Maunachira River which flows past Xugana and Camp Okavango into the northern section of Moremi Wildlife Reserve. The *African Skimmer*, a small houseboat for conveying tourists, leaves its white wake on the right.

Like the River Nile in Egypt, the Okavango sustains life in an inhospitable habitat. It is surrounded by the sands of the Kalahari, a dry semi-arid environment with an average annual rainfall of between 500 and 550 mm. The area is ravaged by periodic droughts and has had a particularly bad series of droughts during the last few years.

The region is essentially flat, with the exception of the Tsodilo Hills, west of the village of Sepupa on the edge of the Okavango, the Aha and Kuanaka Hills near the South West Africa/Namibian border, a series of hills to the south of Lake Ngami, and the Gcoha, Gubatsha and Chinamba Hills east of Savuti in the Chobe National Park.

Botswana has an average elevation of 1 000 m. Summer rain falls between November and March when the weather ranges from warm to extremely hot. The humidity of the region is low and the weather between March and November is usually sunny and cloudless. During this period, it is mostly warm during the day but the evenings and early morning can be cool to cold. It is always advisable to pack a warm jacket or anorak when travelling in the African bush, summer or winter. A drop in temperature usually follows a thunderstorm, and if you are riding on the back of an open Land Rover or sitting in a dugout, it can turn quite cold.

The Okavango Delta represents the largest area of surface water in Botswana, which otherwise has very little. However, the outflow from the delta accounts for less than two per cent of the inflow, most of which evaporates either directly or after utilisation by plants.

Over the years, many rumours have been circulated about the waters of the Okavango being tapped, and a major symposium in 1976 dealt extensively with its value as a wetland. A speaker at the symposium, Keith Thompson of the University of Waikato, New Zealand, summed up the conclusion reached: '... the Okavango Delta is a huge natural resource, but its economic potential is not as great as many people imagine.' Yet, as Botswana is a land-locked country with a semi-arid environment, it is inevitable that the waters of this great delta will attract the attention of government officials, developers and agriculturists.

Considering that 84 per cent of Botswana's land surface is covered by the Kalahari sands (in fact, if there was no Okavango Delta, the entire region would comprise only Kalahari sands and woodland), and that much of this is regarded as good cattle country, it is clear how important water is here – not only for human consumption but also for mining and agriculture. Ken Tinley mentioned in a paper in 1978 that 'the waters of the Okavango Delta are going to be used for development, no matter what counters are raised'.

The important point to consider is that the delta cannot remain an isolated environment for the benefit of tourism alone. It must be managed properly so that it can continue to function as an efficient system capable of supporting both its plant and animal life, and providing the communities of the region with water. Overexploitation of the delta, be it in the form of tapping the water, developing tourism or culling its wildlife, must be carefully monitored and controlled.

Islands come and islands go as the floodwaters of the Okavango rise and fall with the seasons. Permanent islands are marked by tree growth, from wild date palms and strangler figs to sausage-trees and the imposing African ebony.

The Okavango Delta is the principal stronghold of one of the three subspecies of the lechwe, the red lechwe (*Kobus leche leche*). They are almost exclusively grazers and feed on a number of species of semi-aquatic grasses.

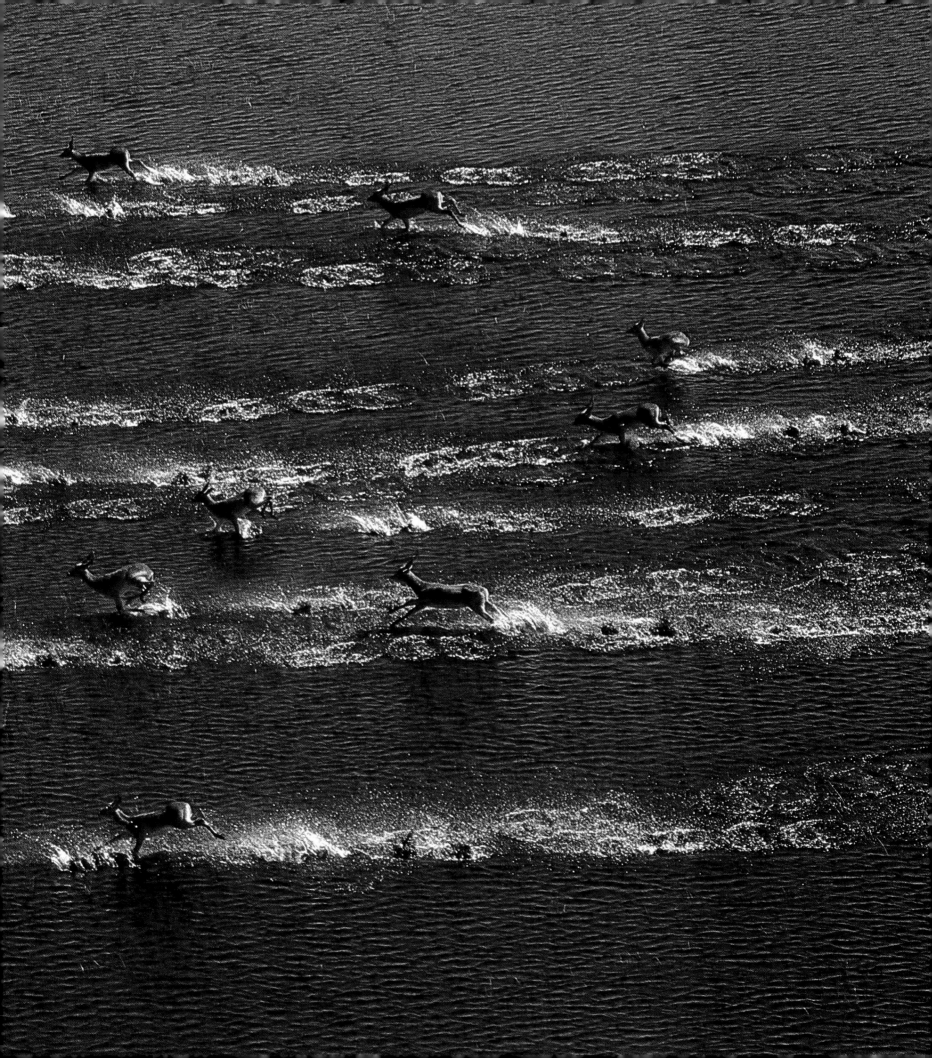

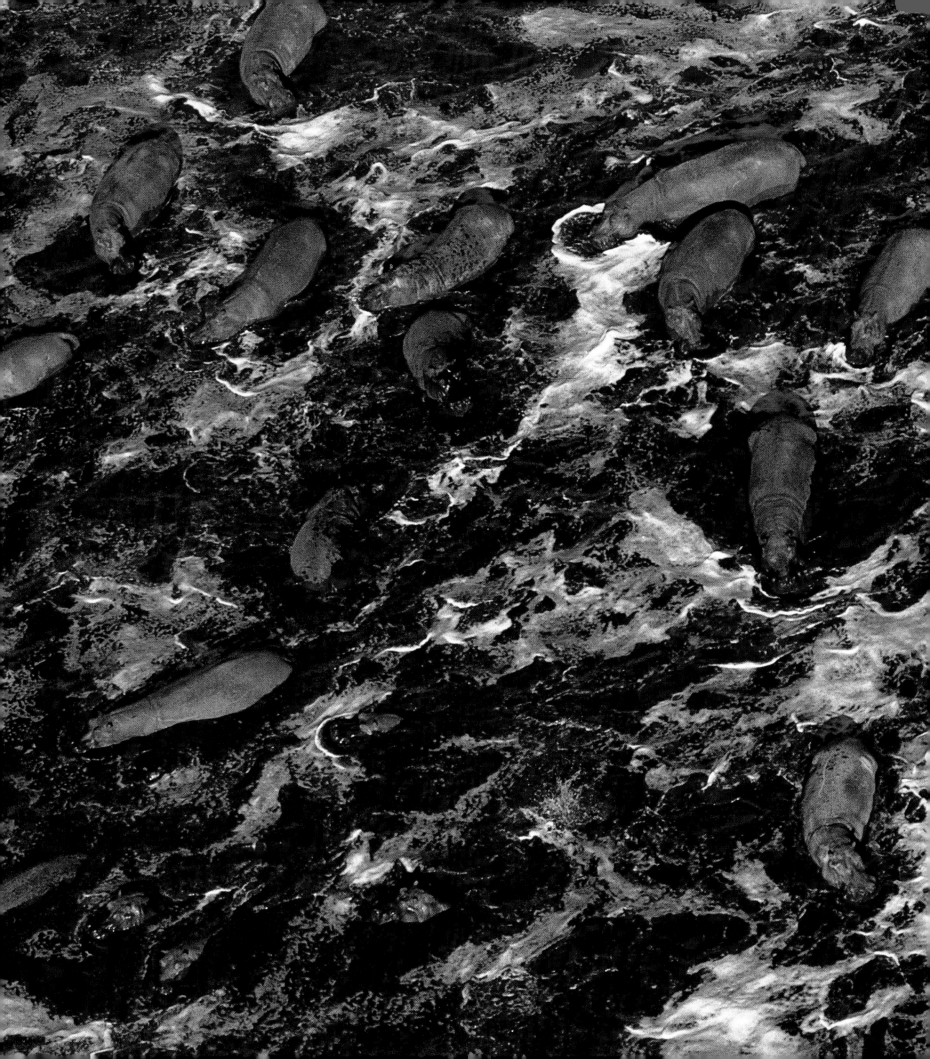

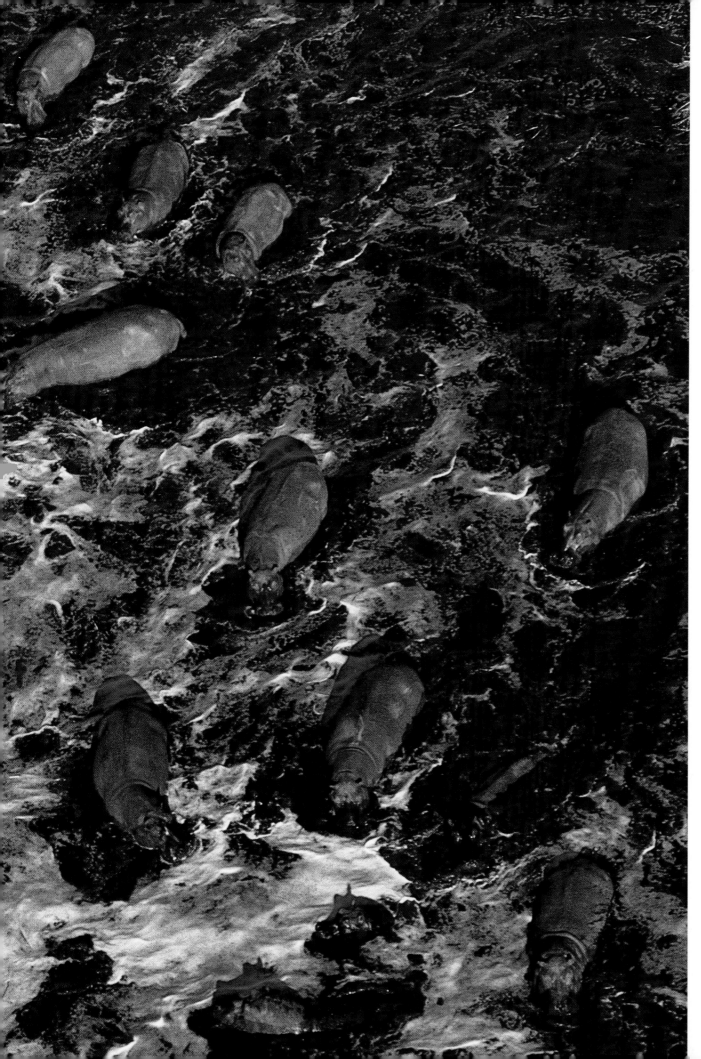

The shallows of the upper Savuti Channel boil as a large school of hippo surges into deeper water. Although hippopotamuses are still relatively common throughout the region, their numbers have declined in the western parts of the delta partly from hunting for their highly prized meat and partly because they are considered a threat to the *mekoro* (dugout canoes) which ply the waterways. These leviathans of the river perform an important function in the life of the swamps, however, keeping the channels clear of vegetation and scattering their dung in the water to the great benefit of the plants and animals living there.

To this end we should bear in mind the words of Ann Crittendon (1975):

'Like a modern Midas, it [tourism] has transformed much of the world's natural beauty into pure gold. In the process, the industry may have planted the seeds of its own destruction. For the suspicion is growing, ever so slowly, that the more tourism succeeds, the more it cannibalizes the very basis of its existence − the wilderness, the unspoiled landscapes, the quaint villages, the unique cultures that drew visitors in the first place.'

The Okavango system is not a true swamp as it has so often been labelled and which label still persists to this day. It is a complex interconnected system, which seasonally floods and spreads out, occupying most of the 15 000 km² of wetland. These floodwaters are usually shallow (less than a metre deep), interspersed with deep channels and lagoons, and dominated by aquatic vegetation. Here as elsewhere in the world the Okavango wetlands are often referred to mistakenly by uninformed people as wastelands.

The delta system plays an important rôle in the lives of African people and supports a rich diversity of animal and plant life. Unlike most wetlands which undergo seasonal fluctuations in water level, the Okavango Delta is different in that its fluctuations are out of phase with the normal summer rains, its seasonal flooding beginning only in the autumn, when the water has completed its 1 000-km journey from Angola.

Acting as conduits out of the delta wetland are the drainage rivers − the Nhabe, the Thamalakane and the Boteti. The former leads to the presently bone-dry Lake Ngami, while the Thamalakane discharges into the Boteti which flows firstly to Lake Xau and, finally, to the giant salt pans of Makgadikgadi. Historically, all these systems were interconnected and included the Linyanti and Chobe drainages of which the Savuti and Mababe wetlands were a part.

This then is the Okavango Delta, an area not only of pervasive beauty and natural splendour, but also one of the most valuable and important wetlands in the world.

The buffalo is found in large numbers in the delta. Although normally occurring in herds of between 70 and 200 animals, they often congregate into enormous herds of up to 1 000 individuals towards the end of the dry season. Their preferred habitat during the rainy season from November to May is the sandveld, rich in nutritious fresh grass. But as the grazing deteriorates in autumn, the buffalo herds move to the mosaic of islands and *melapo* (floodplains), seeking cover by day on the tree-fringed islands and emerging at night to feed and drink on the floodplain.

Following page: The main channel of the Okavango River meanders lazily as it enters the delta south of Seronga, creating a green watery world over the deep sands of the Kalahari. The graceful curves of the 'clover-leaf' at the right of the picture are a well-known landmark for the pilots of light aircraft.

CHAPTER TWO

THE UPPER DELTA AND TSODILO

The Okavango is the third-largest river in southern Africa, entering Botswana at Muhembo. It then follows a fairly straight path to Shakawe, a small settlement situated on the west bank on a bend in the river. From the air, the cluster of white buildings flanking the great river is startlingly bright in the sun. For kilometres on either side of the river the bush stretches out in endless waves of changing browns, which finally disappear in a smoky haze towards unseen horizons. Our aircraft banks away to the left and we come around in a 180-degree turn. Down below, we can see goats wandering through the scrub, and in the distance a plume of dust rises from some labouring vehicle. Groups of people are gathered on the west bank of the river and we see an occasional dugout moving across the water.

Shakawe takes its name from the Hambukushu word for a medicinal tree. Here is the northernmost camp in the Okavango Delta, the Shakawe Fishing Camp, run by Barry Pryce and his wife, Elaine. At this point the river is deep and the banks are heavily wooded in parts. The fishing is good and, as one may expect, birdlife is outstanding. Catching tiger-fish is the main attraction here and provides excellent sport from August to November; you can catch bream too from April to November.

The river, lined with thick groves of papyrus (*Cyperus papyrus*), is up to four metres deep and provides a perfect environment for crocodiles. Venturing into the dark green inlets or rivers for a swim is dangerous, and local inhabitants still fall prey to crocodiles. Lloyd Wilmot, son of the crocodile-hunter, the late Bobby Wilmot, normally has no hesitation in plunging into the waters of the Okavango, but he avoids swimming here.

Large-scale commercial crocodile hunting started in the Okavango in 1956, and over the next 14 years, thousands were shot by hunters up and down the delta. These hunters also pursued their prey along the courses of the main drainage rivers: the Boteti, which flows to the Makgadikgadi; the Thamalakane and Nhabe rivers near Maun; and the Xudum and Thaoge rivers on the west side of the Okavango. This hunting spree has left its mark on the area, depleting the crocodile population quite noticeably in certain places. Crocodile and hippo and other wildlife species are also likely to suffer as more people move into the area. For the present, however, there are enough crocodiles to ensure their sur-

Cutting clear trails through the dense masses of lily-pads in a seasonally flooded *molapo*, Bayei guides propel visitors in *mekoro* into an enchanting world of tiny frogs, gaily coloured spiders, water-birds and tree-covered islands.

The delta supports a wide diversity
of large antelopes, from tsessebe,
kudu, impala, blue wildebeest and
sable to the water-loving sitatunga,
reedbuck, waterbuck and lechwe. Of
these possibly the most
conspicuous is the lechwe, here
plunging through the shallow waters
of a *molapo*.

vival, and in recent years permission has been granted for the capture of several live crocodiles for translocation.

The upper panhandle still provides the best sanctuary along the Okavango River, with the inlets leading to large lagoons and backwaters. I have seen many giant crocodiles in the 10 years that I have flown over this area.

When I started wilderness trails back in 1978, I asked P. J. Bestelink, then owner of the Xaxaba Camp on the Boro Channel, which flows down the west side of Chief's Island, about the quantity and size of the crocodiles there. He smiled and replied: 'We are friends with the crocodile.' I heeded this as a warning not to bathe in the fast-flowing channel or deep lagoon in front of his camp.

Over the years, we got to know where the big ones were and always took precautions when swimming, often using the wooden dugouts as protection. The fact that crocodiles here lack competition because their numbers are low and they therefore have sufficient natural food may explain why more people have not been taken.

One night, while trying to spear bream off the back of P.J.'s fishing boat, I fell overboard, and suddenly found myself treading water in total darkness with only the spear in my hand. This was a terrifying experience.

Hippos, once abundant throughout the region, have been hunted steadily since the Bayei arrived in the 18th Century. Human settlement, pushing down the Okavango River from

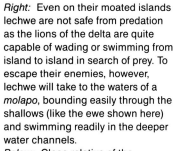

Right: Even on their moated islands lechwe are not safe from predation as the lions of the delta are quite capable of wading or swimming from island to island in search of prey. To escape their enemies, however, lechwe will take to the waters of a *molapo,* bounding easily through the shallows (like the ewe shown here) and swimming readily in the deeper water channels.
Below: Close relative of the hartebeest, the tsessebe appears ungainly but can achieve high speeds with its lumbering gallop and is reputed to be the fastest antelope in southern Africa. It is frequently encountered in the central delta and is a common sight in and around the Savuti Marsh.

The most aquatic of antelope, the sitatunga is magnificently adapted to life in the swamps. It spends most of its time in dense papyrus or phragmites reed-beds in water up to a metre in depth. It walks with ease on the slippery bottom mud aided by its extraordinarily long (16-18 cm), widely splayed hoofs, and is an excellent swimmer. When alarmed or wounded it is said to submerge completely with only its nostrils above water. Only the rams carry horns – spiralled in similar fashion to those of its relative the kudu.

Once abundant, the delta's crocodile population was heavily reduced between 1953 and 1968 when an estimated 50 000 were cropped by commercial hunters to satisfy the demands of international high fashion. The population is now showing signs of recovery, and crocodiles may once again be found in permanent water throughout the delta, as well as in the Linyanti Swamp and along the Chobe River.

the north, particularly down the west side of the delta, has brought increasing pressure to bear on hippos. Not only is their presence considered a threat to river traffic – mainly to the dugouts which ply the waterways – but their meat is highly prized by the Bayei and Hambukushu.

On a number of occasions, hippos have attacked dugouts carrying tourists along the waterways down the Boro Channel, and people and luggage have ended up in the river, with resultant injury and loss of property. Afterwards, the hippo is usually destroyed – an unfortunate result of man's increasing contact with the delta.

Today, the east side of the Okavango, the Kwando-Linyanti and Chobe areas afford the best protection for hippos.

In 1960, at Bobby Wilmot's urging, the then Regent of the Batawana people, Mahumahadi Elizabeth Moremi, banned

the hunting of hippos. This was because they kept the channels open and the water flowing. Without the hippos opening passages through the vegetation, boating would have been quite impossible.

Beyond Shakawe, the river twists and turns down the panhandle flanked by impenetrable banks of papyrus and reeds (*Phragmites mauritianus*). This riverside vegetation serves as home to the shy, seldom-seen sitatunga (*Tragelaphus spekei*). Known as the *naku*, this retiring animal of the upper delta is larger than its relative, the more common bushbuck, and has a similar sharp bark, although more drawn out.

When threatened, sitatunga may immerse themselves in water with only their noses visible. They swim well, and their distinctive, elongated hoofs enable them to move easily over marshes or swamps. They are hunted by crocodiles and

humans but often escape by swimming into deeper waters. Active both by day and by night, sitatunga are usually only seen in the late evening or early morning unless they inhabit undisturbed areas.

The late Bobby Wilmot hunted crocodiles for three years before he saw his first sitatunga. However, with the crocodile population diminishing, their numbers have built up significantly. You won't easily spot a sitatunga from the air because they usually inhabit the most impenetrable, unpopulated areas. Sighting one of these beautiful creatures in the delta ranks with seeing a Pel's fishing owl (*Scotopelia peli*), a large, rufous-brown bird, which is usually found in pairs and hunts for fish in the thick, well-forested riverine areas of the delta's backwaters and lagoons. These owls are largely nocturnal and spend the day camouflaged by the dense foliage

of large trees, occasionally perching on the thick fronds of the giant palm fan (*Hyphaene petersiana*), which the Bayei call the *mokolane*. However, increasing human disturbance is driving them out of their old haunts in some places.

People are often disappointed by the apparent lack of bird life along the Okavango River, especially in areas of dense reed and papyrus. However, some 30 km south of Shakawe Fishing Camp, a superb colony of carmine bee-eaters occupies a sheer bank on the east side of the river.

André, our pilot, increases power and we start climbing to an altitude of 1 000 m above the river. The air is cool up here and we no longer bounce up and down. Only the noise of the engine and the air rushing into the open door breaks our concentration. André cuts the power, turns the aircraft, and now all we hear is the sound of the wind as we glide down

Stalking purposefully through the floodplain marshes the spectacularly coloured saddle-billed stork is a common resident of the Okavango Delta. It feeds on small fish, frogs, small mammals, birds, reptiles and even crustaceans.

Following page: A lone bull elephant wades through the shallow water adjacent to a slow-flowing channel in the heart of the delta. Game-trails criss-cross the inundated grassland, chosen habitat of lechwe, sitatunga and waterbuck.

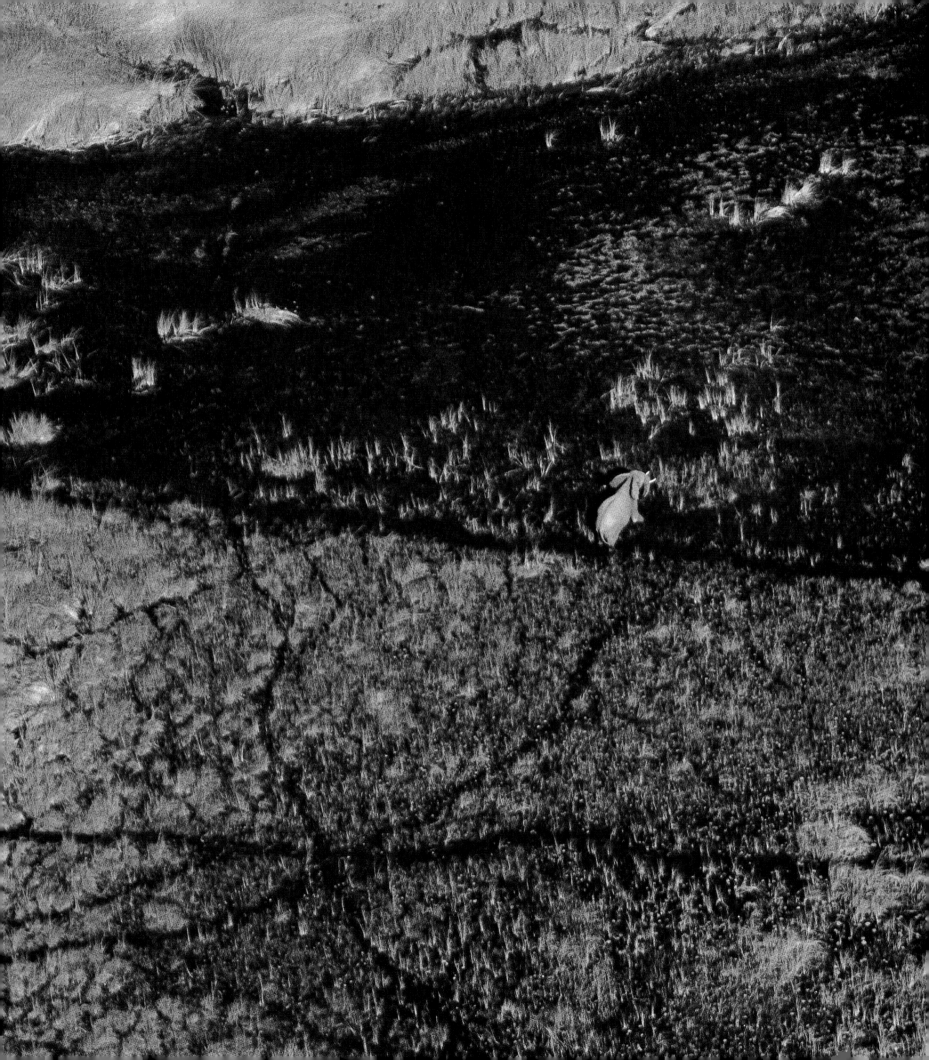

gently and effortlessly. The Okavango Delta stretches out all around us to the distant horizon. Below and behind us the river snakes its way through a maze of tangled vegetation which merges gently with the browns and yellows of the dry thornveld. The unfolding panorama is indescribable and no one speaks – we are overwhelmed. There is little evidence of man's presence down below, but occasionally, here and there, we discern patches of cultivation and clusters of huts. Far off to our left is Kwando-Linyanti, and smoke from various fires is a distant signal of man's presence. The motor-drive on Herman's camera starts winding off again and André applies power. The moment is gone, but the vision remains. We keep our fingers crossed that Herman has captured it on film.

You can see human settlement down both sides of the panhandle to the village of Seronga in the east. South-east of Seronga there is little habitation. However, more people have settled in the west and one is immediately aware of this. From the air we see cattle immersed in water up to their bellies, feeding on the aquatic vegetation; nearby, buffalo and lechwe graze contentedly.

A veterinary cordon fence, protecting the delta from encroachment by humans and livestock, extends around the east, south and west of the delta to a position opposite the settlement of Gumare in the sandveld area on the west side of the delta. The Government plans to extend the fence, commonly referred to as the 'buffalo fence', but this will not include the panhandle.

Much has been written about the cordon fences of Botswana and I will not elaborate on them here. However, this particular fence does offer the best guarantee for the long-term survival of the delta.

As the Okavango River continues its way down the panhandle, it changes course and moves from the eastern side across the papyrus and reeds to the west. It twists and turns gracefully, through constantly changing patterns of green. As we soar overhead, sunlight flashes up occasionally – a constant reminder that the dense green mass of vegetation below conceals water, not solid ground.

We are flying at an altitude of less than 70 m and we see the surface of the water and the reeds rush past at what seems an incredible speed. We have doubled back from Seronga and are heading upstream for Nxamaseri. It was here, between Nxamaseri and Shakawe, that I was first introduced to the Okavango River in 1980. We set off by motor-boat then and spent the entire day travelling to and fro, enjoying the isolation and lack of human habitation.

On the western side of the delta is an old river system which once flowed from eastern South West Africa/Namibia

Somewhat incongruously the sun's rays are reflected from a sheet of water through the smoke of one of the thousands of fires which scorch up to 75 per cent of the delta's surface each dry season.
Coincidentally, however, the floodwaters from the Okavango River's Angolan catchment flow into the delta at the height of the fire season, rejuvenating the *melapo* and bringing new life to the swamps.

past Tsodilo Hills and into the Okavango River. Called the Xeidum Valley (*xeidum* is the Dzucoasi word for 'large river valley'), it now forms a backwater of the Okavango. Here, on the edge of the delta, is the beautiful fishing and bird-watching camp of P. J. Bestelink and his wife Barney. The camp is named after the two lagoons known as Nxamaseri, which are situated where the 'fossil' valley reaches the water. It has a superb position and its environs are frequented by thousands of water-birds in spring. Herons – especially white-backed night herons – darters, pygmy geese, spur-

winged geese, wattled cranes, Pel's fishing owls, Ethiopian snipe, pink-throated longclaws and hundreds of other species may be found.

Further south, past the village of Sepupa and then on to Guma, is the Bestelink's second camp which, in addition to birding and fishing, offers horse trails.

Guma Lagoon (which is more correctly an oxbow lake) is one of the delta's most beautiful places. Here Barney and P.J. have built a lovely rustic camp from mopane poles, reeds and thatch. As we approach from the air, we see a short

runway that ends in the lagoon. André isn't taking any un-necessary chances, so he makes a low-level pass over the runway to check that no stray cattle are about. He pulls the plane up in a gradual, climbing turn and I can see cattle below, feeding on the floodplain beyond the lagoon. Vegeta-tion, freshly slashed and burnt, indicates that this is where wilderness and human habitation merge. The sight jars our senses; so too do the buildings and vehicles that go with such developments.

A lone saddle-billed stork flies below us and as we cross over the lagoon, the sun is a bright orange ball in a cloudless sky. We catch a fleeting glimpse of a sitatunga as the thud of locking wheels prepares us for the landing.

'Bush flying', especially the way we are flying, requires skill and concentration. One is constantly on the lookout for large birds, and the surface of bush airstrips can sometimes be pretty bumpy. Wild animals crossing the runways pose another hazard. You also have to contend with the heat, which can be very uncomfortable – especially if you take off at midday and have a full load of passengers. On one occa-

Bathed in the late-afternoon sun, the brooding and mysterious rock-masses of the Tsodilo Hills rise abruptly from the monotonously flat sandveld some fifty kilometres west of Sepupa. Called by the Bushmen the 'Bracelet of the Morning', the outcrop consists of four hills, the largest being known as the 'Male' Hill while the next two in size are the 'Female' and 'Child' respectively.

Above: This neat Hambukushu village lies about one and a half kilometres west of the Male Hill at Tsodilo. Archaeological evidence suggests that man has lived in this place for more than 30 000 years, but not necessarily continuously. In the past the people obtained their water from permanent springs in the rocks but nowadays have a more certain and accessible supply from a bore-hole.

Below: A small community of Bushmen of the Dzucoasi tribe also lives at Tsodilo, in the shadow of the 300-metre-high Male Hill. They have cast off their nomadic life-style and no longer follow the game herds, preferring instead to cater for the needs of visitors by providing guiding services to the rock paintings or by selling authentic Bushman artefacts such as bow-and-arrow sets and necklaces of ostrich egg-shell beads.

sion, it appeared as if we would run out of runway, but André juggled the aircraft into the air, skimming over the reeds a few metres below.

A short, steep descent, full flaps, over the threshold of the runway and we touch down, bouncing once over the uneven ground before rolling to a stop. We are met by Barney, her camp manager and two large Rottweilers. We unload our gear and soon are having tea on the veranda of the lodge which lies hidden behind two large strangler fig trees (*Ficus thonningii*) – known also as *mu-mu*s. One of the trees is entwined around a *mokutshumo* (African ebony or jackalberry – *Diospyros mespiliformis*) and will eventually take over completely and strangle it.

By now the sun has set and the wind has died down. The delta comes alive with the sounds of early evening and the waters of Guma Lagoon start changing colour. Dusk is short, but just before the light finally goes, a strange last glow – quite unique to the African bush – seems to pervade the entire lake. Suddenly, the moment is gone, and the night descends to the melodious sound of frogs whose gathering chorus competes with numerous insect noises. Mosquitoes are soon about, and we retreat to take a shower.

Later, with a cold beer in hand, we sit around a fire P.J. has prepared and discuss the day's flying, the fish-farming which P.J. is attempting, and how difficult it has been to keep the otters from eating all the bream fingerlings. The fingerlings have also been preyed on by hamerkops and kingfishers which have a knack of finding gaps in the fingerlings' pro-tective netting. Inevitably, the subject of the delta comes up and we discuss its future.

No lions or hyaenas are heard on this side of the delta – man's presence drove most of them out long ago. No doubt they still exist, but there can't be many left.

Eventually we retire to the comfort of two-bedded huts overlooking the lagoon. Dawn finds us up and about and preparing the aircraft for the day's work.

Before leaving the panhandle, you cannot ignore the Tsodilo Hills, a fascinating outcrop of micaceous quartzite schists that rises abruptly from the flat surrounding countryside, due west of the village of Sepupa. Very little surface water is to be found out here in the dry season and game is sparse, although roan and small groups of elephant have been seen occasionally. The tree cover stretches endlessly to the South West Africa/Namibian border.

Tsodilo's dry, hot, brooding, mysterious rock masses rise up some 300 m above the flat plain as our aircraft approaches from the east. Lloyd Wilmot has flown across from Savuti to accompany us on this trip as he knows the Tsodilo well. The Bushmen call the outcrops the 'Bracelet of the Morning' and have named the three largest of the four hills, the Male, Female and Child respectively.

History does indeed surround this place, which has been occupied by man for more than 30 000 years. Among those who have lived in its shadow have been communities of both Bushmen and Bantu.

Two ancient riverbeds, the Xeidum and the Tamacha, pass

To the Bushman the Tsodilo Hills are a place of myth, magic and mystery. Over 2 700 magnificent rock paintings have been discovered there but both the Hambukushu and the Bushmen deny any knowledge of who the original artists might have been. Although it is almost certain that Bushmen were the painters, the Dzucoasi at Male Hill attribute these works of art to their god Gaoxa.

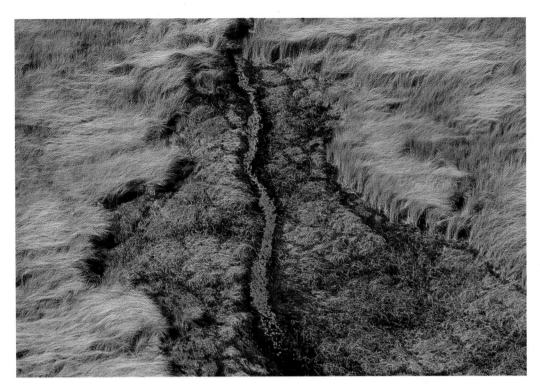

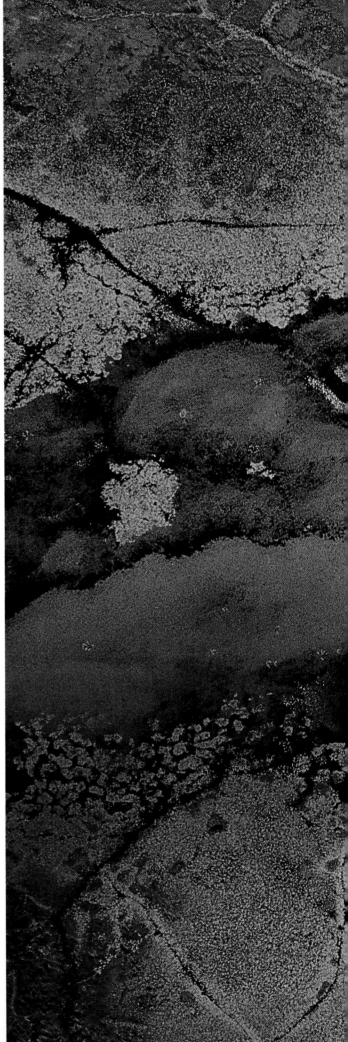

Above: An emerald carpet of water-lily pads marks the path of a narrow water-channel as it winds sinuously through a stand of tall grass – some of which has been ravaged by fire.
Right: Mokoro channels form an interlacing tracery through the water-lilies of a lagoon at Chief's Island in Moremi Wildlife Reserve in the central delta.

to the north and south-west respectively. Formerly they flowed towards the basin of the present-day Okavango Delta. There are a number of permanent springs in and about the hills which a small band of surviving Bushmen and the Hambukushu once relied on for water. They now draw their water from two wells.

Our aircraft passes the Male Hill to the west as we turn on to our downward leg for a landing. Below us dense woodland rises up to the base of the hills and we feel the heat coming up to meet us.

Herman is photographing through the open doorway as the aircraft is rocked by turbulence. Lloyd points out salient features of the hills as I take copious notes and my son Anton occasionally passes a roll of film across to Herman.

Two vultures whizz past to the left and right as André skilfully flies between them. The wind howls into the open cockpit as we turn to land. The wheels are already lowered and locked into place, and André pushes the 210 Centurion down against the heat. Herman is still taking pictures; we are captivated by the ground rushing forward beyond the open door. We touch down and roll to the end of the runway. A battered, dark-green, abandoned Land Rover is the only evidence of man that awaits us. Watching it there in the shade of an acacia tree, you imagine it saying: 'I've travelled all this way through this cursèd land, only to wind up forsaken in the shadow of these hills.'

Maun is some 350 km away – at least a 12-hour journey in a four-wheel-drive vehicle. If you are thinking of making the trip to the Tsodilo Hills, be forewarned: no facilities exist there so you would be well advised to be fully equipped before setting out.

Lloyd sets off along a well-worn path and we race to catch up with him. Soon we come to a small Bushman settlement.

Right: Guests from Xugana Lodge on the Maunachira River north of Moremi Wildlife Reserve fish in the placid waters of a lagoon. Like the Bayei and Hambukushu, the tourists fish for bream and catfish, but the sport-fishing prize *par excellence* is that sleek, ferocious predator, the tiger-fish.

A scene in the main delta south of Guma Lagoon. The Swedish hunter/traveller Charles John Andersson said of the Okavango Delta in 1853: 'On every side, as far as the eye could reach, lay stretched a sea of fresh water, in many places concealed from sight by a covering of reeds and rushes of every shade and hue; whilst numerous islands spread out over the surface and, adorned with rich vegetation, gave to the whole an indescribably beautiful appearance.'

the soft Kalahari sand makes the going tough as we climb up the track between the Male and Female hills to the first painting depicting the rhino. The sand, which once formed ancient dunes here, has been stabilised by vegetation with the passage of time. There is much to see in and about these hills, and the views across the Kalahari are breathtaking both in summer and winter. An aura of mystery surrounds the place, dominated by a silence that broods in the shimmering heat.

The Bushmen of the Dzucoasi tribe are permanent settlers here now, having cast off their nomadic life-style. No longer do they follow the herds of game, preferring instead to make bow-and-arrow sets and artefacts for the tourists. Old women busy themselves preparing food, or offering us souvenirs; others just sit chatting to one another. Dogs, looking close to starvation, wander in and out of huts, their ribs jutting out of loosely hanging skins; chickens of various hues and shades are all about, sticking their heads in pots, scratching the

Above: To many people, the strikingly handsome African fish-eagle epitomises the Okavango. It spends much of the day perched prominently in trees, occasionally soaring down to stoop at fish 15 to 30 centimetres below the surface of the delta's clear waters. The pads on its feet are equipped with small spicules which, together with the long claws, allow the fish-eagle to obtain purchase on even the most slippery of fish.

Left: Cantering through the shallow waters on the edge of Guma Lagoon, a cheerful group of riders led by Barney Bestelink sets off on a horse-trail – a novel and exhilarating way to explore the Okavango Delta.

Above: Clouds build up over Xugana Lagoon – one of the delta's largest – at the start of the rainy season in November. The *African Skimmer* houseboat, with an upper deck over four metres above the water, operates out of Xugana Lodge, giving visitors to this part of the northern delta a unique giraffe's-eye view of the wildlife beyond the tall waterside vegetation.

Right: Most of the lodges or camps in the delta are off the beaten track – if track there is at all – and tourist access is usually by light aircraft. Visitors arriving at Guma Lagoon Camp's airstrip (right) can step off their plane on to the banks of Guma Lagoon.

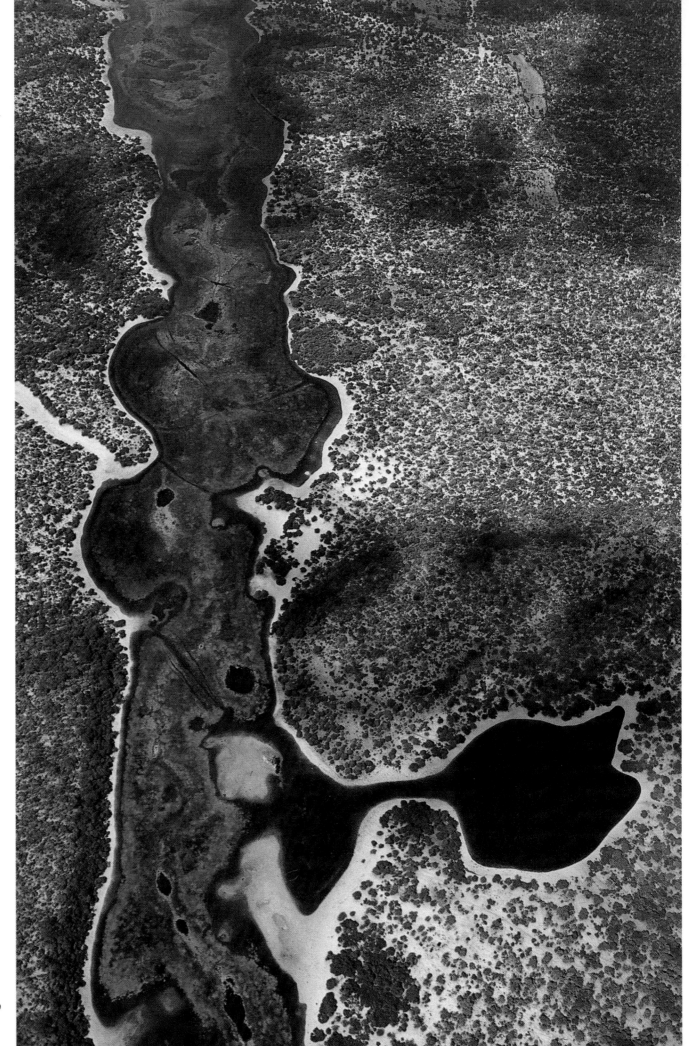

In the upper reaches of the 'panhandle', where the Okavango River crosses the Caprivi Strip and enters Botswana, the river is confined to a narrow channel and possesses virtually no floodplain. Beyond the tree-fringed banks of the river the arid, lightly wooded Kalahari sands stretch away to the horizon. At its March/April peak, when the Angolan floodwaters arrive, the river will carry 1 600 cubic metres of water per second; at its lowest level in November, however, it may carry only 150 cubic metres per second.

ground unconcerned. Some of the elders are well into the twilight of their lives and none of us can guess their ages.

Tourism alone has brought civilisation to Tsodilo, and I cannot help but feel a sense of sorrow at the life-style which has overtaken these Bushmen. They have tried to adapt to a changing world, but sadly it has left them behind. Their forefathers, who have long been locked away in the sands of the Kalahari, knew the hills and their secrets well.

Taking off from the dusty airstrip at Tsodilo, our aircraft makes a right-hand turn to gain height and to come around parallel to the Male Hill. It looks massive and beautiful in the late afternoon light, with the sun shining on its western face. Suddenly, an upthrust of air shakes the aircraft violently.

André concentrates on controlling the plane, Herman swears, and the rest of us hang on. After that, we stay away from the hills and climb quickly. The air is cool and calm as Tsodilo grows smaller in the distance, and we head for Savuti via Guma to collect Lloyd's aircraft.

After landing at Guma, we waste no time in taking off again and set a course for home on the edge of the Savuti Channel. It is dusk now, so we cross the sand ridge and prepare to fly straight in. A few bull elephants stand motionless around the main water-hole, their trunks limp; warthogs scamper away with tails erect; over to our right on Harvey's Pan, a lovely line of giraffe moves along slowly and gracefully, disappearing in the gathering darkness.

As the river progresses down the 'panhandle', its floodplain widens and by the time it reaches Nxamaseri it has become a magnificent and complex spectacle of perennial and seasonal swamps with a myriad of wooded islands large and small.

Chapter Three

LIFE IN THE DELTA

We will leave flying for a brief spell and cover this chapter on foot and by dugout to look at the scene from the ground.

The Okavango Delta comprises three major ecosystems, distinguished by their relative lack or abundance of water. In the first part of our story, we dealt with the area of deep, permanent water in the far north. The second ecosystem is seasonally inundated. The extent of this inundation depends largely upon the annual flood from Angola, and the amount of the summer rains. In this region – the lower delta – are hundreds of islands covered by dense, riparian woodland. The larger islands also support open grassland, woodland and an occasional baobab tree. The third ecosystem consists of the higher, dry land areas. A good example is Chief's Island, which lies roughly in the centre of the delta and forms part of the Moremi Wildlife Reserve.

On the eastern side of the panhandle where the delta begins to fan out is the main Bayei village of Seronga (meaning 'whirlpool'), whose tidy reed and thatch homes flank the deep waters of the Okavango. The flowing river curves to such an extent here that it almost doubles back on itself, forming a breathtakingly beautiful 'clover leaf'.

Life for the people of the delta revolves closely around the river whose seasonal flooding is crucial to the success of their annual crops and the grazing of their cattle. The floodwaters, which reach the central and southern region between June and August, have started receding rapidly by September, enabling the inhabitants to plant in saturated ground. The summer rains, which usually start in November, now provide the moisture needed for growing crops. The people of the Okavango are fortunate, therefore, in having two types of fields for growing crops: *masimo a bokgola* (floodplain fields) and *masimo a pula* (rain fields), thereby benefiting from flood- and rain-water respectively.

The historical migration of the Bayei and Hambukushu people, who came to the Okavango from Zambia, is inextricably tied to the ancient drainage systems of the Zambezi, Chobe and Okavango rivers. Whenever these systems flooded, they became linked to one another, enabling these people to settle and travel about the region. During the past hundred years, however, the alteration and drying up of the watercourses has severed the link between the systems.

The largest single group living in and around the delta are

The late afternoon sun elicits autumn colours of gold and auburn from the woodland at the eastern end of Moremi Wildlife Reserve near Khwai River Lodge.

Above: November rains have drenched these reed-thatched huts on an island on the west side of Moremi Wildlife Reserve. Xaxaba and Delta camps employ their staff from villages such as this and, by doing so, inject much-needed cash into the local economy.

Right: Thunder-clouds rumble ominously in the sky over Moremi Wildlife Reserve at the start of the rainy season. These first spring rains herald the annual dispersal of elephant, zebra and other large game animals out of the delta to the rejuvenated vegetation and rain-filled pans of the Kalahari sandveld.

the Bayei, the first Bantu-speaking people to migrate here from an area west of the confluence of the Chobe and Zambezi rivers. Their settlement is believed to have started earlier than the 18th Century; in fact, it is possible they may have occupied parts of northern Botswana for more than a thousand years.

They made their way into Ngamiland in dugouts and on foot, and first settled around Lake Ngami; thereafter they moved into the delta, probably attracted by the abundance of fish and hippo there. Some time after their arrival, they had so successfully penetrated the delta that they could boast: 'We are like the flies that float in a milk pail.'

It is quite likely that the Bayei travelled to Lake Ngami via the Selinda Spillway, a broad shallow channel which links the Chobe and Okavango systems and which carries over-flow water to the Chobe during peak flood. They may also have travelled via the Savuti Channel to the Mababe Depres-sion (then a large lake), coming down south along old river-courses to the Thamalakane River, the Nhabe River, and then on to their final destination, Lake Ngami. They were later followed by the Hambukushu who first settled in the Kwando-Linyanti area. Today the Hambukushu may be found along the entire length of the Okavango panhandle in the north. They are known as the 'deep-water people', being very much at home in the deep waters of this part of the Okavango Delta.

The Bayei and Hambukushu were not the original inhabi-tants of the Okavango, having been preceded by the Banoka, the 'people of the river', often referred to as the 'river Bush-men'. The latter, however, are ethnically related to the Bantu people and not to the Bushmen, and they speak a Hottentot dialect of Khoe. These people have been associated with Okavango for a very long time. Their origins are unknown,

but they are believed to have lived along the Boteti River and to have penetrated the delta, settling along the edges of the channels and on the islands. They later learnt from the Bayei how to make and use dugouts, and this enabled them to penetrate still further into the delta where they lived successfully as hunter-gatherers. The Bayei were mainly hunters and fishermen, while the Hambukushu were excellent crop-farmers. Both raised domestic stock.

This then is a brief history of the early settlement of the delta by the Bayei, Hambukushu and Banoka people.

No journey to the Okavango is complete without travelling by mokoro (plural *mekoro*), the dugout fashioned from some of the delta's most spectacular trees, including the African ebony or jackal-berry and the sausage tree (*Kigelia africana*). Constructing a mokoro can take up to six weeks. Using a *selepe* – a type of axe shaped like a hoe – the canoe is carved out from a solid tree trunk. Trimming is effected with a *petwana*, an adze. The completed mokoro is then carried and floated back to the village where it is submerged for a while in water alongside the landing-stages to ensure that it doesn't crack.

Today, the same flat-bottomed mekoro, which enabled the early Bayei to penetrate the delta, are commonly used for travelling, hunting and fishing. In the past decade they have been used more extensively for taking visitors along the incredible waterways of the Okavango. Unfortunately, the increasing demands of the tourist industry here are taking their toll on the trees which are used for making mekoro.

I started conducting wilderness trails into the delta in 1978, and every time I have set out, the same feeling of excitement has enveloped me. The central Okavango, with its

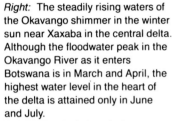

Right: The steadily rising waters of the Okavango shimmer in the winter sun near Xaxaba in the central delta. Although the floodwater peak in the Okavango River as it enters Botswana is in March and April, the highest water level in the heart of the delta is attained only in June and July.
Below: Tourist lodges in the Okavango Delta do not cater only for the wealthy – some are designed specifically for low-budget visitors. Oddballs is one such camp which attracts younger spirits in search of high adventure by *mokoro*, while the nearby Delta Camp, shown here, offers more expensive facilities.

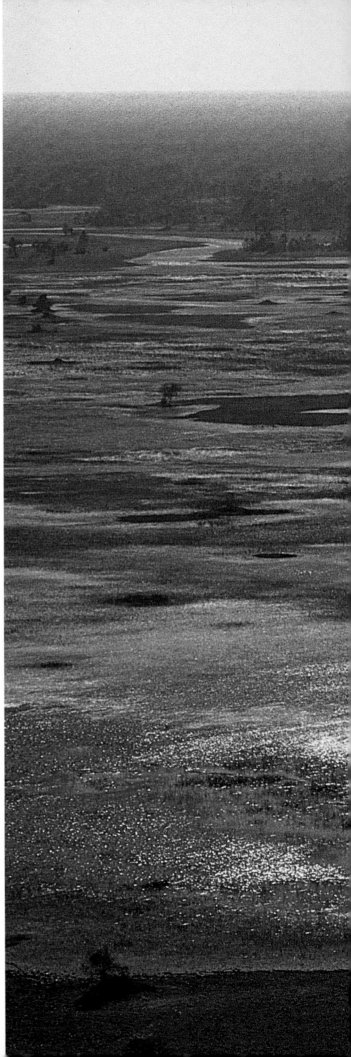

A sturdy thornbush stockade surrounds this cattle kraal near the village of Gumare on the western edge of the delta. Lions and spotted hyaenas are still a very real threat to the cattle-based economy of the Bayei villages and it is the task of young boys to guard the cattle by day and to herd them into the safety of the kraal by night.

hundreds of islands covered by beautiful trees, its *melapo* (seasonally flooded areas – singular *molapo*), its channels and lagoons, has lured visitors from far and wide. Straddling the whole of this vast area is Chief's Island, some 50 km long and 10 to 15 km wide – the largest permanent dry land mass in the heart of the delta. Totally uninhabited by humans, it is the home of numerous species of large animals, notably buffalo and lion. To the west of Chief's Island, the Boro Channel bears much of the Okavango's flowing water on its southward journey. Some distance north of the island of Chao, the Boro becomes the boundary of the Moremi Wildlife Reserve as far south as Nxaraga Lagoon.

There are a number of fine lodges here, including Xaxaba, established by Lloyd Wilmot, Delta Camp, a short distance downstream from Xaxaba, and Mombo in the Jao Concession, north-west of Chief's Island. These camps, along with most of the region west of the Boro Channel, are controlled hunting areas run by private safari companies. They provide luxury accommodation in a rustic setting, giving you the option of living in the delta in comfort, or roughing it on a wilderness trail.

A wilderness trip into the Okavango Delta is taken by mokoro with Bayei guides. Leaving the aircraft at Xaxaba Camp's airstrip, we make our way to the small landing-stage on the edge of the Boro Channel, where Saraxô, our Bayei guide, greets us. We drink a cold beer while the Bayei guides start to load personal baggage, chairs, lunch and cameras. All the camping gear is already loaded into the baggage mokoro. The water here is crystal-clear, fairly deep and swift-flowing. It is July and the flood is reaching its peak at Xaxaba. Tall reeds line the banks and numerous water-lilies are clustered around the six mekoro preparing to depart. It is warm and everyone has changed into shorts and bathing costumes.

Birdlife is abundant and our group is eagerly engaged in identifying various species. A fish-eagle calls clear across Xaxaba Lagoon amidst the laughter and chatter of our party.

Before we leave, I introduce my group to our guides and fill in with a brief history of their origins. Saraxô, as lead guide, is anxious to begin the four-hour journey to the island he has chosen for the night.

The group is advised about bathing and crocodiles, and told how to relax in a mokoro; one must not fidget or get up, especially in deep water. The dugouts are pushed out into the main stream and we set off in single file. My dugout leads and is followed in the rear by our baggage craft. The finest way to relax tired, overworked city-dwellers is to transport

A buffalo herd makes its way across a shallow river between Guma and Gumare in the north-west delta. The buffalo of the delta and the domestic cattle on its fringes are prevented from mingling by the Buffalo Fence, an enormously long game-proof fence which cuts a swathe around the western and southern borders of the Okavango. Erected some years ago by the Botswanan veterinary authorities, its purpose is to ensure that the highly contagious foot-and-mouth disease is not transmitted from the buffalo (in which it occurs naturally) to the cattle of the Kalahari (which are highly susceptible), as this would place Botswana's important beef exports to Europe in jeopardy. The fence, however, not only protects the cattle from disease, but also has the effect of safeguarding the wilderness and wildlife of the delta from competition with cattle and the encroachment of civilisation.

A fire crackles fiercely through a phragmites reed-bed next to a deep water-channel in the heart of the delta. Usually set by hunters, such fires clear the floodplains of vegetation and make access by *mokoro* easier. Game animals are attracted to the fresh green shoots that spring up after fire, and fall ready prey to the hunter's gun.

them into the Okavango by dugout. Once accustomed to the rhythm of the current and the abrupt tilt as the mokoro turns, they start to settle down.

We leave the deep water as soon as possible, for here we are at our most vulnerable to capsizing and perhaps encountering a hippo, known locally as a *kubu*. Once a hippo confronted my baggage dugout late one afternoon, causing the paddler to head straight into a reed- and sedge-covered island where he stayed for three hours – too afraid to proceed for fear of an attack. My party and I had passed the same spot some time ahead of him without incident. I figured the hippo must have been in a side lagoon.

A week later, one of my South African guides, Ian Walker, and Motsumi, our Bayei head delta guide, encountered the same hippo, this time with more serious consequences. The hippo surfaced behind their mokoro. Lunging at the vessel, it started biting at the rear end; this sent the three occupants flying into the water, and the cameras, binoculars and other valuables went to the bottom. All three scrambled onto the edge of the hippo grass growing alongside the Boro and from there to dry land. Although the Bayei guide cut his leg, and various items were lost, the dugout was recovered a little while later, and all was well

Because hippos have posed a threat to mekoro on the west side of Chief's Island, many of them, sadly, have been shot. Historically the Bayei have always hunted hippos. Not only is the hippo the Bayei totem, but hunting it has been regarded as an important politico-religious performance relating to authority, rain-making and initiation. To kill hippo the Bayei used a type of harpoon called a *chirra*, which consisted of a small barbed spear attached to a wooden shaft. This in turn was secured to a rope. A hunting expedition required the co-operation of several people and was not only exciting but dangerous, with the hunter sometimes becoming the hunted, and ending up seriously injured, or worse. A large raft or *huzhenje* made from papyrus reeds was built and a mokoro was laid on it at the front and centre, with the hunters in the rear. The entire force then floated down a channel into a peaceful group of hippos. Once in their midst, the men stood up on the raft and plunged their harpoons into one of the unsuspecting animals. They then pushed the mokoro off the raft and into the water. Amidst all the confusion and noise from the wounded hippo, the hunters then tried to reach the bank, struggling to hold on to the ropes which were attached to the harpoons embedded in the hippo's back. Upon reaching the bank, the Bayei hunters se-

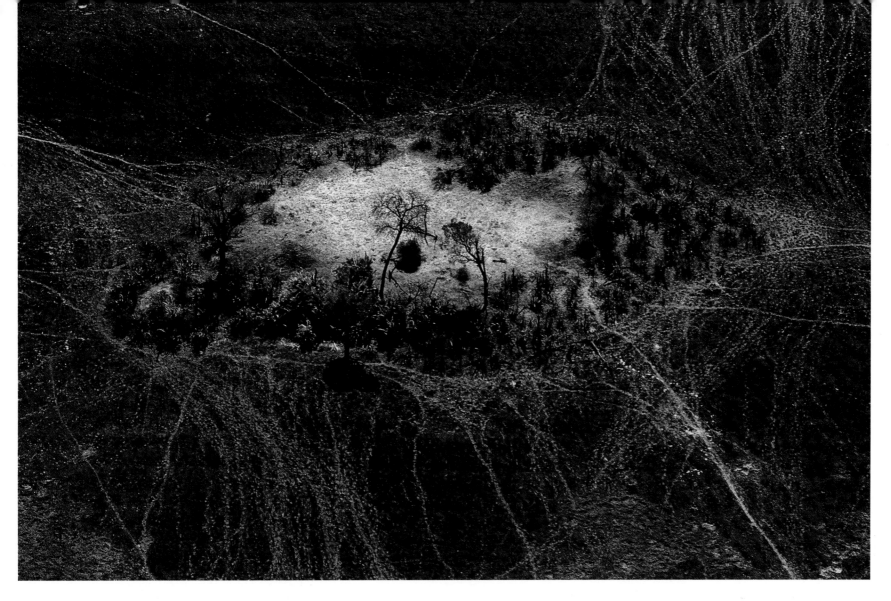

cured the ropes to trees and then used heavy spears to stab the now exhausted animal. It is not surprising that the hunters were sometimes seriously injured or killed – a wounded hippo can be very dangerous.

Late in the afternoon, after an uneventful journey from Xaxaba, we near our destination – a camp-site on one of the hundreds of islands on the edge of a molapo. After leaving the mainstream, we turn off into the narrow channels flowing through this molapo. The channels, made by dugouts, hippo and buffalo, are less than half a metre deep in places. As we push ahead, numerous beautifully coloured spiders and reed-frogs slip into our dugout. These little creatures alarm the city-dwellers at first, but they get used to them remarkably quickly.

Now and then, our guides stop to point out reedbuck, lechwe, giraffes or warthogs. Birdlife here is prolific and includes the often-seen wattled crane, and the rarer slaty egret (*Egretta vinaceigula*). The Okavango is a bird-watcher's paradise, with 400 recorded bird species. Various operators run special 'bird trips', undertaken on foot, in mekoro or on houseboats. A special attraction for bird-watchers are the noisy heron breeding colonies on the small islands in Gcodikwe Lagoon.

Surprisingly, waterfowl are not well represented, although spurwinged geese (*Plectropterus gambensis*), white-faced ducks (*Dendrocygna viduata*) and pygmy geese (*Nettapus auritus*) are common. This may be owing to the fact that the pattern of flooding causes a lack of suitable niches for waterfowl, and also that the Okavango River carries very little organic or mineral matter into the delta, resulting in fairly low levels of nutrients in the system.

Often seen in the delta are raptors, the most common of which is the African fish-eagle (*Haliaeetus vocifer*). You will see this beautiful bird in the vicinity of channels and among the riverine vegetation fringing the islands. Bateleurs are also abundant.

A variety of large trees and bush fringe the islands, which increase in number towards the south. These trees, particularly the Lowveld mangosteen or *motsaudi* (*Garcinia livingstonei*), impart a protective and peaceful embrace to travellers setting up camp for the night.

Having arrived at our island, Arrilechwe, we start putting up camp; this means clearing a spot to sleep, lighting a camp-fire, laying out sleeping-bags, hanging up mosquito nets and unpacking luggage and food. Meanwhile, one or two Bayei are busy setting out their nets to catch fish.

The aftermath of a fire east of Chief's Island in Moremi Wildlife Reserve. This tree-fringed islet is surrounded by a sea of charred vegetation, traversed by a web of game-paths. When the floodwaters rise again in autumn and winter, the *molapo* around the islet will be transformed once more into a shallow lake, alive with fish and frogs, water-birds and insects.

'New water' from the rising Okavango River spills into the parched Kalahari sands on the western edge of the delta near Gumare. This annual miracle of water flooding the Okavango basin under cloudless skies is one of the wonders of the natural world.

There are around 65 species of fish in the delta and Lake Ngami. While about 20 per cent of these may have some commercial value, overfishing in the many *madiba* (lagoons) and backwaters of the panhandle and western areas is a real problem. Tiger-fish (*Hydrocynus forskahlii*) are much sought after today by sport-fishermen, while the Bayei and Hambukushu fish for bream (*Tilapia* spp. and *Oreochromis* spp.), silver catfish (*Schilbe mystus*) and catfish (*Clarias* spp.). Fish-eagles are always at hand in nearby trees, hoping for a free meal.

As dusk settles, the mosquitoes arrive; now you know you're truly in Africa. After a good meal and a beer or two, you forget about the mosquitoes, and before long turn into warm sleeping-bags under mosquito nets. The low, distant moan of a lion, the occasional whoop of a hyaena and the cough of a leopard remind you that the delta is home to an extremely wide variety of large and small animals. Leopards are common and widespread in Ngamiland today, but in 1964 a report in the newsletter of the Fauna Conservation Society of Ngamiland said it was feared that they might be nearing extinction in the Moremi Wildlife Reserve.

Although the Fauna Conservation Society's report also said that vultures − 'once such a characteristic feature' − were seldom seen, we saw them constantly from the air, and

often had to take evasive action to avoid them. Once, while we were collecting material for this book, a vulture rose up at great speed on a thermal and collided with our aircraft's right wing.

The permanent delta sustains only three large animal species − crocodiles, hippos and sitatunga. More than 20 large mammal species, however, occupy the dry land areas and the seasonally inundated areas. Buffalo are by far the most abundant species in the central delta, but zebra, tsessebe, impala, giraffe, lechwe, waterbuck, reedbuck, elephant, sable and roan are just a few of the wide diversity of larger mammals which can be seen there, not to mention a host of smaller animal species.

Crocodiles head the list of reptiles which occur in the delta. Two species of monitor lizards or leguaans (*Varanus niloticus* and *V. exanthematicus*) are also found throughout the region. The largest snake is the African rock-python (*Python sebae*), and the most dangerous is the black mamba (*Dendroaspis polylepis*).

On our island we rise before dawn and drink steaming coffee as the sun rises above another island nearby. Later we set off again in our dugout, and as we glide through the water, a tiny lily makes a watery sound as the poler puts his *nkashe* stick in and drags the lily's bulb beneath the surface. The

'Dust devils' swirl over the dry burnt grasslands of the western delta, carrying dust, smoke, leaves, seeds and even small creatures high into the air. Created by thermals, these powerful whirlwinds in miniature are a common sight in the early winter before the floods arrive.

Bayei call these lilies *muxobu* from the sound they make as they disappear beneath the water.

Off to the east a smoky haze hangs in the air – the result of one of the countless fires that have raged throughout much of the dry season. Hunters are usually responsible for these fires which greatly influence the movement of the delta's wildlife, and no doubt affect the delicate ecology of the system. The destruction of vegetation by fire often enables the water to gain access to areas it would not normally reach, and gives polers an easier passage in their dugouts.

We spend much of the day on foot carrying our food with us. Drinking water is readily available. We spend the next few days marvelling at the Okavango's wildlife; there is ample time for bird-watching, studying the ecology of the delta, stalking zebras through the long grass, and watching the antics of those common inhabitants, the baboons.

We get to know the Bayei guides and learn a lot from them. They show us how to follow honeyguides to bees' nests, how to make rope from the bark of baobab trees, and how to track big game. They play music on a *warra warra*; this is a bow-shaped musical instrument with a taut string which, held over a cupped mouth, creates sound from its various vibrations. The string is fashioned from the fronds of the mokolane palm (*Hyphaene petersiana*).

The days and nights slip by in the delta, and time means nothing here. Before we know it, we have to return to Xaxaba Camp.

Left: Only fifty kilometres west of the flooded flats of Nxamaseri in the Okavango 'panhandle', the Tsodilo Hills serve as an unmistakable landmark for aircraft pilots and on a clear day can be seen from more than 100 kilometres away.
Below: A grotesquely fat baobab squats at the edge of a flooded *molapo* near Nxamaseri in the Okavango 'panhandle'. A wealth of myth and superstition surrounds these extraordinary trees – one tale being that God planted them upside-down. The wild date palm in the foreground bears an edible sweet fruit in summer, beloved of birds and fruit-bats.

CHAPTER FOUR

THE SOUTH-EASTERN DELTA AND LAKE NGAMI

To many visitors Xaxaba is one of the really well-appointed camps in the Okavango. It is situated on the edge of a lagoon and has its own airstrip, as do most of the other delta camps. The only way to get to any of these camps quickly is by air, and all of them are served by various organisations flying people in and out. Many camps have their own aircraft which will pick you up and transport you directly over the delta.

Shortly after taking off from Maun, you cross the veterinary cordon fence and see the vegetation change completely as the water stretches out ahead for hundreds of square kilometres. Nothing can prepare you for this breathtaking panorama, especially at the height of the floods.

It is about 15 minutes from Maun to Xaxaba and soon the aircraft starts to descend. Burnt areas stand out grey and black against the pale yellows and browns of the grassy islands. Dark vegetation surrounds the water's edge and the mokolane palms are conspicuous with their pale grey-green fronds and dark, long trunks. You can see fish-eagles sitting in trees on the edge of a molapo or flying below. Over to our right is the dry landmass of Moremi, and between Xaxaba and the second camp in this area, Delta Camp, we see a large Bayei settlement with dozens of thatched houses. It is from such settlements that the camps draw their work force, especially the paddlers who transport you into the Okavango Delta. Both Xaxaba and Delta Camp cater for modern-day explorers seeking to venture into the Okavango. They also provide rustic accommodation for the less adventurous.

Before long, the aircraft is down and rolling towards the welcoming party. The dense vegetation covering the edges of the channels and lagoons often camouflages the camps, and the buildings come as a surprise after the short, hot flight from Maun. Once on the ground, you may be struck by the abundance of birds which the camps seem to attract. From your camp you can explore the waterways and islands by motor-boat or dugout canoe for as long as your visitor's permit allows.

After our sojourn at the camp, our aircraft lifts above the trees and water of Xaxaba and we head eastwards towards Savuti and Chobe. We cross over Chief's Island and into the east side of Moremi Wildlife Reserve. This forms part of the dry landmass which also includes the sandveld tongue west of the Boro River.

A caravan of buffalo wends its dusty way through the russet, winter-dry grasses and reeds of Moremi Wildlife Reserve in the Okavango Delta. The sandveld is the buffalo's preferred habitat but as the rain-water pans dry up in early winter the herds move to the *melapo* for water and grazing.

Following page: Tall phragmites reeds dwarf a herd of buffalo as it treks purposefully to water.

Right: Like cavalry regiments on manoeuvre, two herds of buffalo sweep over the flat parkland of eastern Moremi raising a thick cloud of dust. Dry-season congregations of buffalo can number up to a thousand individuals.
Below: A herd of sable antelope gallops off through long grass in Moremi Wildlife Reserve. The bulls in particular have an almost heraldic appearance with their glossy jet-black coats and perfectly curved, swept-back horns.

The Moremi Wildlife Reserve was established in March 1963 at the request of various residents in Ngamiland. By incorporating Chief's Island in 1976 its area was extended to 3 880 km². Administered by Botswana's Department of Wildlife and National Parks, the reserve today is a tribute to the Batawana people who understand the long-term importance of preserving wildlife. You can visit Moremi's well-appointed camps and lodges by road or aircraft. These camps, including Camp Moremi, Khwai River Lodge, Tsaro, San-ta-Wani and Camp Okavango, are household names in the delta, offering hospitality and beautiful surroundings.

A group of bull elephants, belly-deep in a marshy backwater east of Chief's Island in Moremi, feeds on aquatic vegetation and reeds oblivious of the aeroplane overhead. Elephants spend up to 18 hours a day feeding, in which time they will consume between 250 and 300 kilograms of green food and around 150 litres of water.

83

Buffalo bulls cool off in a shallow pan green with algae near San-ta-Wani Safari Lodge on the east side of Moremi Wildlife Reserve. Mud-wallowing tends to be a male indulgence and buffalo cows and calves usually stand or lie in the dappled shade of woodland or reed-bed to escape the midday heat.

The ecological diversity of the reserve is superb. Dense mopane woodland, interspersed with large stands of acacia woodland are characteristic of the area. The reserve's eastern boundary borders the eastern edge of the delta and here you can view the pans, lagoons and vleis from a four-wheel-drive vehicle. Designated camp-sites are to be found within the reserve and at the two entrances to the sanctuary. The presence of hippo here makes it hazardous to travel by mokoro.

Because many parts of the sanctuary are inaccessible by vehicle or boat, they still remain a vast wilderness area, untouched, and often unseen by man. The wilderness to the north-west of the reserve forms part of one of the hunting concession zones. Here is the beautiful Xugana Lagoon, one of the largest in the delta, and the luxurious, tented camp of the same name.

The lagoons, more correctly referred to as oxbow lakes, or by the Bayei as *madiba* (singular *lediba*), are spectacular features of the Okavango. The eastern side of the delta, from

A school of hippo wallows in the mud of a shallow lagoon in Moremi, basking in the autumn sun while oxpeckers cleanse them of ticks, flies and other invertebrate irritants. Although the hairless skin of the hippopotamus is sensitive to the sun it is protected to some extent by a viscous reddish glandular secretion. Nevertheless hippos never stay for too long out of the water.

Xugana downstream, has some of the most beautiful oxbow lakes, with exciting names such as Xobega, Shindi, Gidikwe, Dashakau and Xaxanika.

On one of our photographic flights we observed the *Sitatunga* houseboat on the beautiful, horseshoe-shaped Xobega Lagoon. Many of the lagoons are off the main channels, fed by narrow streams. They are a refuge for a wide variety of wildlife, including hippos and crocodiles which you may encounter basking on the grassy verges. Many of the crocodiles in this part of the delta are particularly large.

Floating papyrus and reeds fringe the lagoons, and from the air you can see the hippo paths radiating out to their grazing grounds. Lechwe abound in the open clearings away from the lagoons, and you can see saddle-billed storks and wattled cranes stalking through the shallows or across the grey-and-black burnt areas.

Left: Clustered around the carcase of a buffalo, a pride of lionesses refuses to be unsettled by the approach of our aeroplane although one or two voice their displeasure with a snarl. Taking their cue from the adults, the cubs pay little attention to us and continue to feed. *Above:* On our second pass over the kill, the lionesses stared curiously at the plane but soon returned to the serious business of filling their bellies. No male lions were in evidence in the vicinity, no doubt to the gratification of the lionesses who usually do most of the hunting but then have to stand back until the dominant pride male has taken 'the lion's share'.

Previous page: Outpaced by their custodians – two young herd-boys – a flock of goats flees from our approaching aircraft as we fly low over the dry bed of Lake Ngami. The well in the foreground has been dug to provide water for cattle, goats, donkeys and man: there is none to spare for the once-rich wildlife of this dying lake.

Right: Like a swarm of locusts, an enormous flock of red-billed queleas assembles to drink at the shallow channel of the Nhabe River between Maun and Lake Ngami. These highly gregarious relatives of weavers and bishops nest in thorn-trees and reed-beds in dense colonies and are a well-known and much-feared scourge of agricultural seed-crops.

Opposite above: Lake Ngami in 1988 from an altitude of 6 000 feet (2 000 metres). Described by missionary/explorer David Livingstone in 1849 as a 'fine-looking sheet of water' and with an estimated circumference then of 120 kilometres, the lake today is a featureless dust-bowl. In exceptionally wet years, however, it can fill at least partially, when the Thamalakane River overspills into the Nhabe River and when the rivers of the Xudum system overspill into the Kunyere; the Nhabe and the Kunyere together discharge their waters into the Lake near the village of Toteng, transforming the basin into a breathtaking paradise for waterfowl and other wildlife.

Opposite below: Startled springbok bound off across the bed of Lake Ngami. These graceful antelope are well adapted to arid conditions and can obtain all their moisture requirements from the vegetation that they eat.

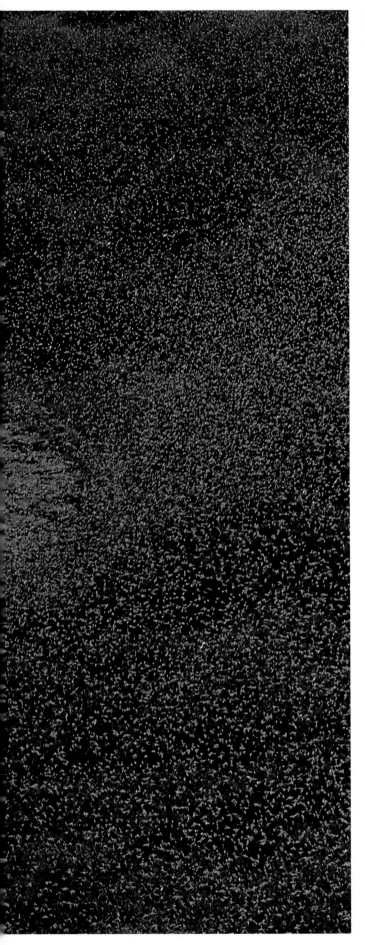

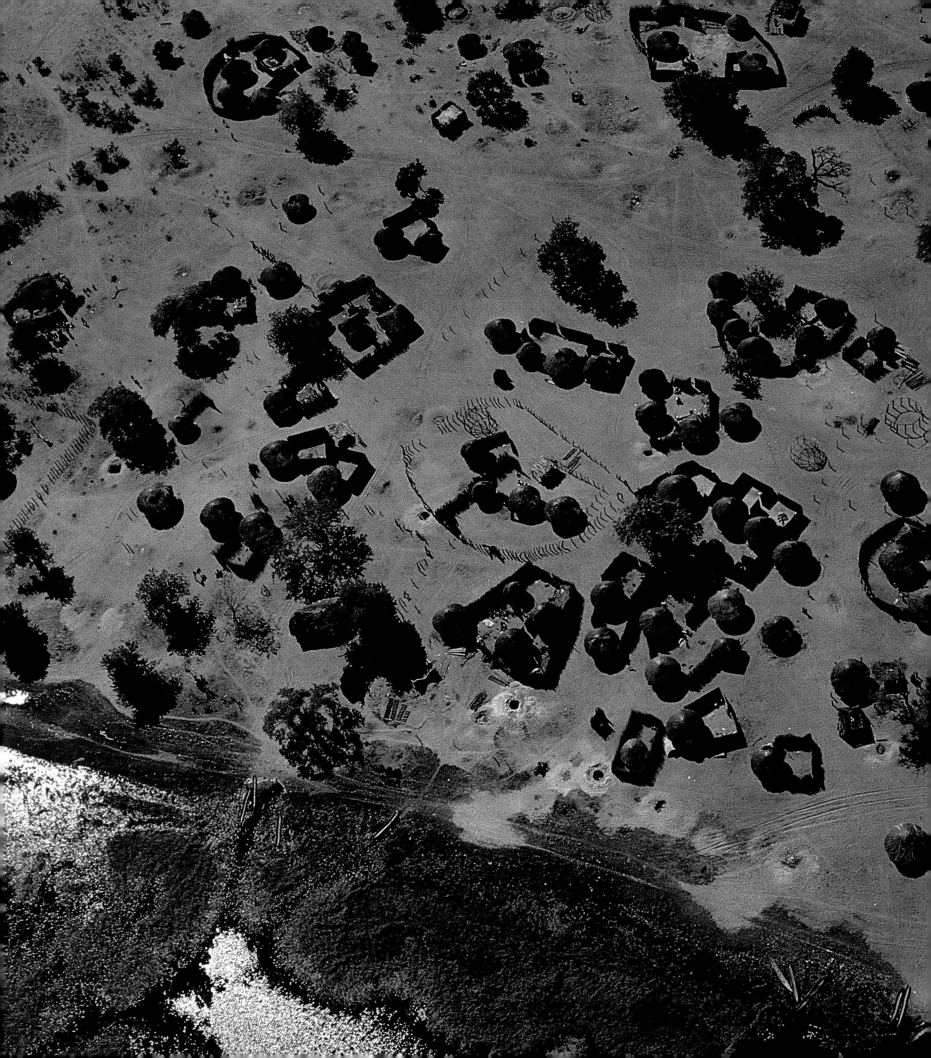

Clusters of trees emerge from small islands; particularly noticeable from the air are the mokolane palms – a major feature of the Okavango. Commonly known as vegetable ivory palms, they bear fruit the size of billiard balls and are eaten with relish by elephants and baboons in October when they ripen. The outer fibrous casing has a guava-like taste, and many a pile of elephant dung is littered with the remains of this fruit from which the outer covering has been removed. A potent alcoholic brew is made from the sap of the mokolane palm and it is frequently tapped wherever it grows in southern Africa, although the practice is not so widespread in the delta.

Growing on the fringes of the islands and lagoons, is the wild date palm (*Phoenix reclinata*) which the Bayei refer to as *tsaro*. This evergreen tree with its cylindrical-shaped stem grows up to six metres, producing a small, orange-coloured, date-like fruit which is eaten by a variety of animals.

Above: Maun, the tribal capital of the Batawana people and administrative centre of Ngamiland, swelters in the heat of the afternoon. A scattering of mopane trees, however, provides shade from the relentless sun.
Left: Sunlight is reflected off the waters of the Boteti River as it passes a village south-east of Maun on its way to the Makgadikgadi Pans. The Boteti carries away the surplus water of the Okavango Delta – a mere two per cent of the volume entering the panhandle at Muhembo, some 275 kilometres to the north-west.

Cattle quench their thirst in the cool clear waters of the Boteti. The river is slow-running and tranquil and provides safe anchorage for the water-lilies and other aquatic plants that are found in greater abundance further west in the seasonal swamp channels of the Okavango Delta.

94

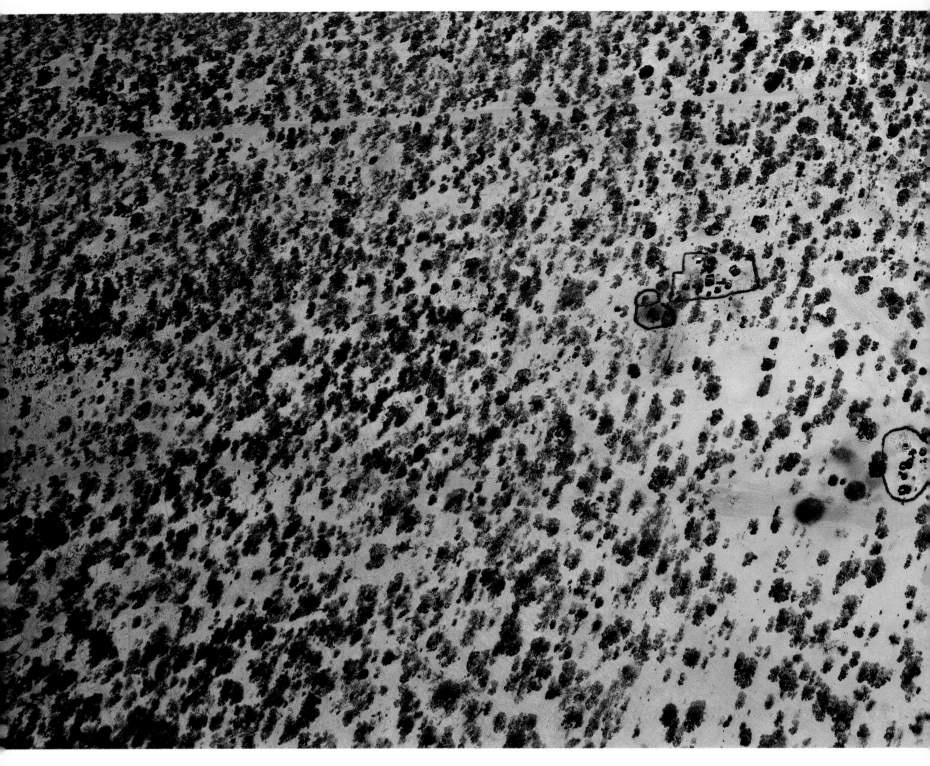

Many of the numerous tree species of the Okavango play an important rôle in the lives of the local inhabitants. The silver cluster-leaf (*Terminalia sericea*), known locally as the *mogonono*, provides the poles with which the Bayei propel their mekoro around the delta. This is a hard, largely insect-resistant wood which is also used in the construction of buildings and for firewood.

Baobab trees (*Adansonia digitata*), or *mowana*, grow on many of the delta's larger islands. Renowned as a source of food and of traditional medicines, the baobab has a soft,

spongy timber with few practical uses although the fibrous bark is used extensively for cord in Ngamiland.

Another splendid tree − one of the tallest found on the islands − is the *mokutshumo* (*Diospyros mespiliformis*). Its hard termite-resistant wood is used for building mekoro. The tree also carries a pleasant edible fruit, relished by animals and humans in spring.

Elephants occur with increasing frequency on the east side of the Okavango Delta; as you move into the drier areas and north to the Savuti Channel in the Chobe National Park,

evidence of their presence becomes more and more apparent. Their trails lead to numerous pans in the area, and you can see the remains of mopane trees – an important source of food for elephants – pushed over in their hundreds.

Botswana has an estimated 40 000 elephants, and their range extends from the Zimbabwean border right across the Okavango Delta. As we fly low over the woodland, we see the elephants in their family groups. Sometimes they ignore us, at other times they race off with trunks raised.

For most of our flights across the vast wilderness, we main-

tained a height of between 100 and 130 metres in order to cause as little disturbance as possible. We never intended to chase any animal, although obviously this was not always possible. An unfortunate aspect of tourism in the delta is the tendency of some pilots to fly low over the region, a practice which can be annoying to visitors on the ground, in a vehicle or in a mokoro – to say nothing of the disturbance caused to the animals.

The extent of the Okavango's diversity of wildlife was well illustrated to us one afternoon while flying down from

A panoramic view of the acacia scrubland immediately adjacent to the Boteti River shows an overgrazed landscape denuded of its grass and herb cover by cattle and goats.

Seronga where we had been filming the 'clover leaf' and the numerous lagoons in the Xugana area. We spotted two lions at a buffalo carcass in tall, golden grass which had been flattened where the buffalo now lay. The shout of 'lions!' had André swinging our aircraft over to port. This was followed by much anxious peering ahead to pick out the animals. Coming round in a tight circle, we could see them clearly on the ground, standing over their dead quarry. One of the lions stared at us curiously, while the other looked towards a group of seven buffalo which were bearing down on them. Whether this was intentional on the part of the buffaloes is uncertain, but it did have the effect of driving the lions off.

As we banked away, we spotted 20 elephants emerging from a pan, and in the distance, towards Linyanti, we could see a huge column of smoke rising from a grass fire. A white-backed vulture swung away to our left; we turned right, and I saw a black crocodile, at least three metres long, basking in the late afternoon sun on the edge of a pan. We often saw them in the small pans and, occasionally, some distance from any large body of water.

Before going on to Chobe National Park and the famed Savuti Channel, let us return to Maun, the gateway to Ngamiland. Here the Thamalakane River drains what is left of the waters of the Okavango Delta – just two per cent of the original input – into the Boteti River. Having taken six months to reach Maun, the flood reaches a peak here in July. The slow movement of the waters of the Okavango Delta, together with their low sediment load, results in the water being crystal clear. The light amber colour of the water is due to the suspension of fine organic matter. The fall in height of the delta is a mere 62 m over its entire length of some 250 km, hence the slow movement of water over many months. Over the floodplains, the floodwaters move at a rate of about three kilometres a day.

Maun, established in 1915, is the tribal capital of the Batawana people. Its name comes from the Bayei word meaning 'place of black reeds'. As the administrative capital of Ngamiland it houses all the various Government departments, and services the hunting and tourism industry of the region. Here most delta journeys begin, whether they are wilderness trails, fishing expeditions, luxury photographic safaris or hunting trips. A smart hotel and some comfortable lodges provide the dusty, tired traveller with a meal and a good night's rest. There are also stores, banks and other facilities. The town still retains its frontier character, and its history is steeped in both the authentic and the apocryphal exploits of its inhabitants. Five kilometres of tarred road run through the centre of Maun.

The Buffalo Fence on the south-eastern fringe of the delta was built to prevent the spread of foot-and-mouth disease from the buffalo to the cattle outside. It also, however, serves to prevent cattle from invading the sanctuary of the central delta. This aerial view graphically illustrates the contrast between the overgrazed cattle range on the left of the fence and the healthy ground cover on the right – a stark reminder of the fate that will befall the delta's wildlife if economics should ever dictate that the fences should be removed.

Above: A cattle drive raises clouds of fine dust south of the Buffalo Fence near Maun as herders accompany their stock in search of pastures new.
Right: Cattle trudge along well-worn tracks to find water during the very dry conditions which prevailed in Botswana in 1987. Such trails stretch for many kilometres over bare sand from which every edible morsel has been stripped by cattle and goats. During the recent drought many thousands of cattle succumbed.

As you approach the airfield from the south, you see hundreds of delightful grass huts, a refreshing change after the concrete jungle of Johannesburg. We land on the airport's excellent tarred surface, refuel and check that we are cleared for our low-level flight down the Boteti River and to the dry Lake Ngami.

There is a perceptible air of excitement as you alight from your aircraft in Maun, the hot dry air making you acutely conscious of the fact that you are now in the heart of Africa. Four-wheel-drive vehicles are everywhere and the people are casually dressed. There is a hum of activity at the airport where a restaurant, shops and the administrative headquarters of the camps and lodges are located.

Contact with the delta is maintained by aircraft and radio, and you will see a constant stream of planes taking off with tourists or supplies to some camp deep in the Okavango. Somehow everyone gravitates to the airfield, for this is the nerve centre of the wildlife industry.

We climb away swiftly in spite of the heat, for our aircraft is lightly loaded with only four of us aboard. Turning to starboard and passing over the Thamalakane River, we can see that domestic stock have had an impact on the countryside, which is so different here to that of the delta on the other side of the buffalo fence. A long line of cattle plods along below us, sending a dense column of dust into the clear sky. We can also see goats and donkeys on the bare veld.

In the past decade drought has had a severe impact on the population of domestic stock in Botswana, reducing the number of cattle from more than 3,5 million to about 2,3 million.

Then on to Lake Ngami, 98 km to the south-west of Maun in the southernmost corner of the Okavango Delta. The lake was seen by William Cotton Oswell's party on 1 August 1849, and Dr. David Livingstone, who was in the party, described it as a 'fine-looking sheet of water'. During the following five years, the explorers Joseph McCabe and Charles Andersson followed in Livingstone's footsteps. All described

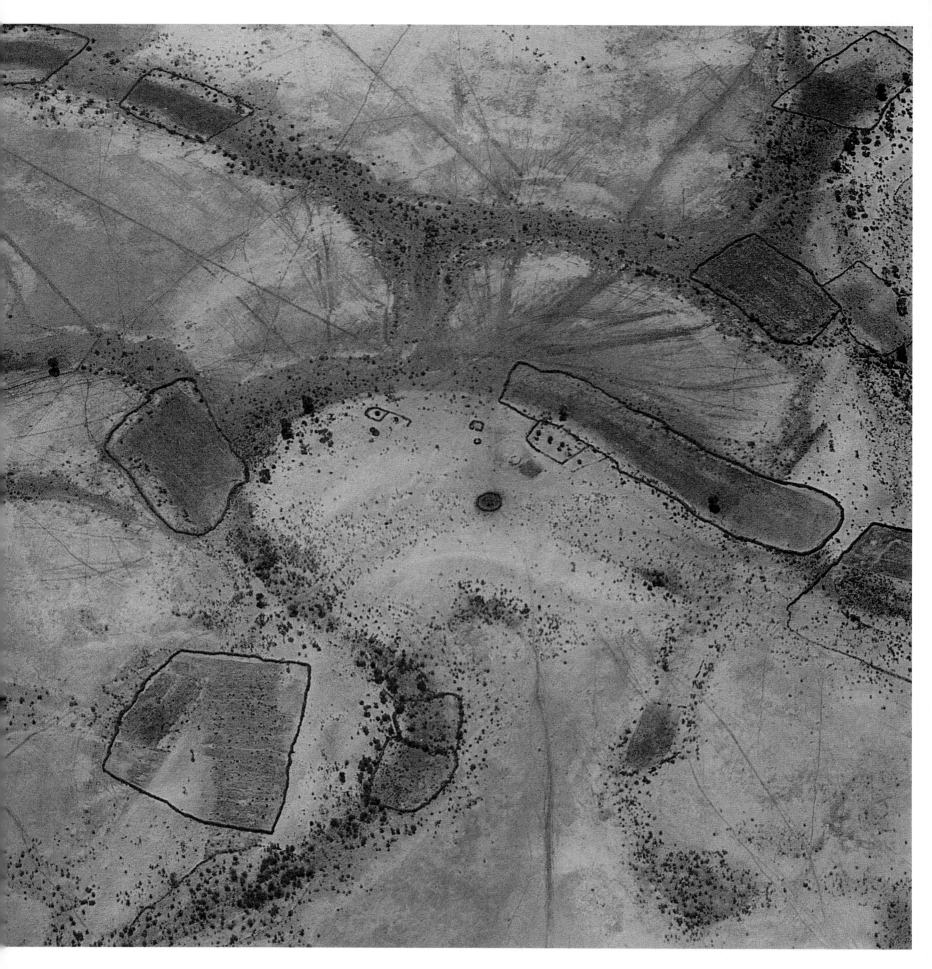

the lake as containing good water, mainly from the Thaoge River which drained down the west side of the Okavango Delta. Hippo and crocodile were abundant in the area in those days and it was a haven for birdlife.

The lake is completely dry today, although it has flooded six or seven times since the lower reaches of the Thaoge River dried up around a hundred years ago as a result either of blockages by papyrus reeds or of tectonic movements of the earth's crust.

Our flight takes us down the tree-lined banks of the bone-dry Nhabe River to the village of Toteng, where it is joined by the Kunyere River. There is a large cattle population in the Lake Ngami area, attracted by excellent grazing when there's water about. In the last few years, the drought has taken its toll of livestock in the vicinity of the lake, which is now littered with the carcasses of dozens of cattle and donkeys.

As we skim low over the dry lake bed, we see deep wells excavated by the locals to provide water for their thirsty animals. The place has a desolate atmosphere; the once vast reed-beds are now dry sand, and only the memory of hippos remains. Once a part of the prehistoric super-lake system, Lake Ngami has shrunk and been cut off with time, leaving it a virtually separate entity.

When water does come to the lake, it transforms it into a haven for birdlife, creating a perfect environment for thousands of waterfowl. Nowhere else in Ngamiland will you see such a profusion of birds. They include white-faced ducks by the thousand, yellow-billed ducks, teal, Egyptian and spurwinged geese, shovellers, knob-billed ducks and shelducks. There is also a profusion of lesser and greater flamingoes, pelicans, marabou and Abdim's storks, herons and ibises. The list is endless and the variety breathtaking as the birds are attracted to the lake's nutrient-rich waters. When Botswana's current drought ends, the return of this incredible community of birds promises to be one of southern Africa's wildlife extravanganzas.

Above: Does the future lie in large-scale irrigation schemes such as this one south-west of Maun not far from the end of the delta? Heavily fenced against both cattle and wildlife – but not against insects – its green luxuriance contrasts sharply with the semi-desert scrubland beyond the reach of pump and sprinkler-system.
Left: Cattle-trails cross the dry, baked earth around the enclosures of a Batawana cattle-post along the Boteti River south-east of Maun. A series of dry years combined with heavy stock pressure has brought the fragile vegetation cover of this region to near-ruination.

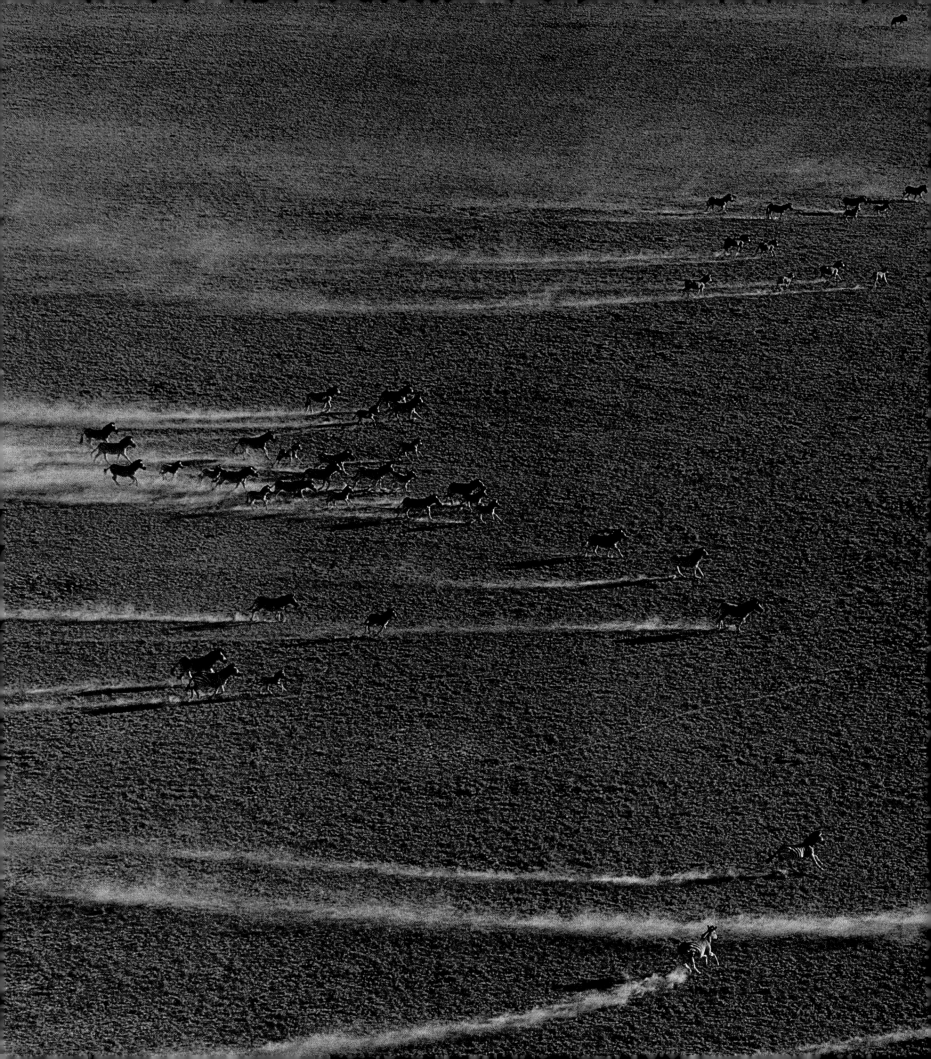

CHAPTER FIVE

MAKGADIKGADI

From a distance, the ground radiates a white light which grows progressively brighter. The air is bumpy as we rise to an altitude of 700 m above the dry, brown Kalahari scrub. We are approaching the famed Makgadikgadi salt pans. Covering an area of thousands of square kilometres, these pans are among the largest on earth.

The glare is intense as we descend towards the centre of the pans, having left the Boteti River where it turns south to the village of Rakops, some 40 km from Lake Xau. The waters of the Okavango finally come to rest here along the Boteti River as it heads towards Lake Xau. By this time, less than two per cent of the water remains from that which originally entered the upper Okavango panhandle; most of this will disappear before it reaches Lake Xau, the last remnants being channelled off by man.

The Makgadikgadi Pans are the relics of a prehistoric super-lake believed to have been one of the largest lakes in Africa, covering an area of about 60 000 km² and which included a large portion of the present-day Okavango Delta.

What are the secrets of these salt-encrusted pans, and where did all the water go? We may never know the full story, but there is convincing geological evidence that all the areas we have covered in this narrative were once interconnected.

Some three million years ago, the Kalahari experienced a period of high rainfall. One or more of the Chobe, Okavango and Zambezi rivers flowed strongly, draining to the southeast into the Limpopo and onwards into the Indian Ocean. A million years later, the region experienced a buckling of the earth's surface, resulting in a fault which is known as the Kalahari-Zimbabwe Axis. The flow of these three great rivers was interrupted, causing them to spill back and fill the Makgadikgadi basin. Further faulting diverted the waters of the Upper Zambezi and Chobe rivers to the north-east, into the middle Zambezi, ultimately forming the Victoria Falls in Zimbabwe and reducing the size of the super-lake. Climatic changes since then, coupled with the eastward loss of water and further geological disturbances, caused the almost complete drying up of the lake.

The Thamalakane fault line effectively isolated the Okavango from the Makgadikgadi, leading to the establishment of numerous isolated pans as the lake continued to diminish. Today the Okavango is the only watery remnant of this super-lake. In the Makgadikgadi, as the water retreated, grass

The thundering hoofs of a cavalry charge of Burchell's zebra raise the midwinter dust on the sun-scorched grasslands of the Makgadikgadi Pans Game Reserve.

Breathtakingly beautiful, the Makgadikgadi Pans stretch in primaeval silence to the horizon. These relics of the great Kalahari super-lake of prehistory are now completely dry for the greater part of the year and only occasionally do good rains in the region permit large areas of standing water to develop. Then, as if by magic, a vast concourse of water-birds appears from nowhere to feed on the sudden — if ephemeral — flourishing of algae, brine-shrimps and other forms of water-borne life.

sprung up in its place, establishing a huge grazing area for the countless thousands of plains game that are today such a spectacular feature of the game reserve.

The horizon is hazy and in the distance the pans seem to merge with the atmosphere. A feeling of timelessness pervades the vastness of these pans, and it is difficult for us to comprehend the huge span of time in which the lake has undergone such radical change.

The Makgadikgadi comprises two pans, Ntwetwe in the west which is the larger, and Sowa which lies to the east. North and west of Ntwetwe Pan are vast, open, grassy plains covered with mokolane palms, which stand out beautifully, like sentinels, in the early morning and late evening light. It is strange to see these trees, which seem better suited to the Okavango Delta, growing out here.

Above: As the summer rains bring life again to the sun-dried Makgadikgadi plains, troops of Burchell's zebra arrive from far and near to graze the fresh new shoots, rich in protein and moisture.
Left: Just to the south of Nxai Pan National Park lies Kudiakam Pan, noted for its group of obese and venerable baobab trees known as the 'Seven Sisters' or 'Baines' Baobabs'. In May 1862 the artist and traveller Thomas Baines camped here and immortalised the trees on canvas. These ancient veterans have hardly changed in appearance in the intervening 125 years.

Not now found in the huge aggregations of yesteryear, springbok are nevertheless still abundant in the arid regions of the central Kalahari and the Makgadikgadi Pans. These handsome antelope are well adapted to the unpredictability of the rainfall of their semi-desert habitat, moving *en masse* to areas where rain has fallen to take advantage of fresh green growth and obtaining all of their water requirements from their food.

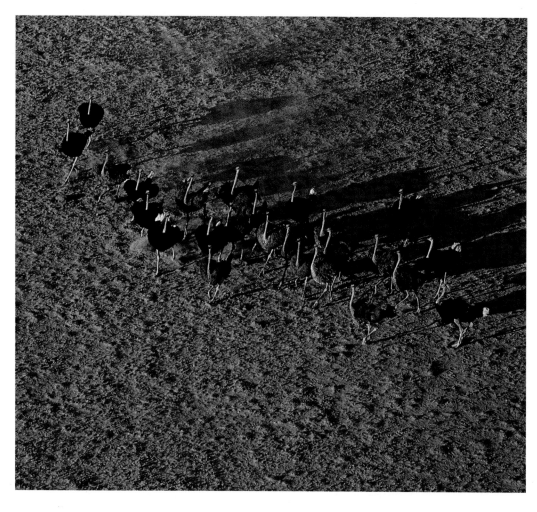

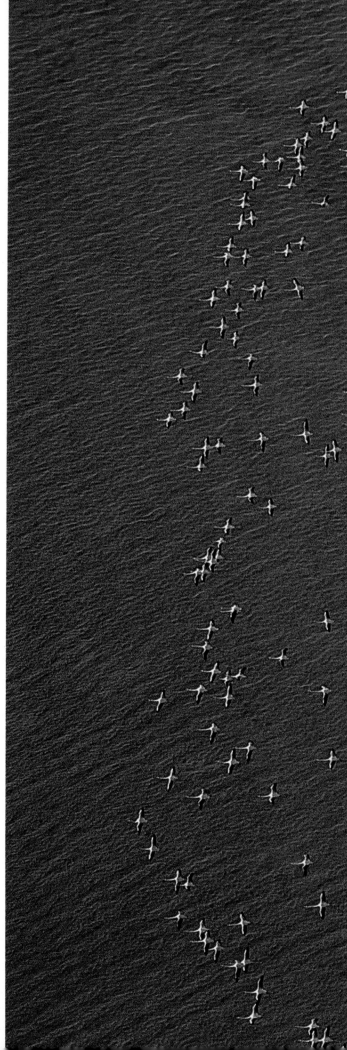

Above: This flock of ostriches appears to be pondering one of the great mysteries of life – that they, the largest living birds, are earthbound, while man in a strange reversal of rôles, flies arrogantly overhead. The cock ostriches may be distinguished from their brown consorts by their jet-black bodies and white wings.

Right: Far below our aircraft a cloud of flamingoes passes over the shallow waters of Sowa Pan, the easternmost of the two great Makgadikgadi Pans. Fed by the Nata River after good summer rains in western Zimbabwe, this north-eastern section of Sowa has attracted tens of thousands of greater and lesser flamingoes to feed on the rich soup of algae, diatoms and myriads of salt-tolerant aquatic invertebrates.

With the exception of an ostrich or two, you are unlikely to see animals on the salt pans, although there are tracks which cross over from one pan to another. Wildlife in Makgadikgadi frequents the edges of the pans and the grass-covered areas which were once inundated with water.

Seasonally, you will see most of the large animal species in the parks surrounding the main pans. These are the Nxai Pan National Park, covering an area of 2 100 km², and the Makgadikgadi Pans Game Reserve, which is 3 900 km². Botanically the area is fascinating and the birdlife is excellent.

Nxai Pan, also once part of the extensive lake system of Makgadikgadi, Mababe, Okavango and Ngami, is a grass-covered plain some 14 km across. During the rainy season from December to March you will see large herds of game here. This is the haunt of lions and cheetahs, giraffes, wildebeest, zebras, eland, springbok and sable. Elephants and buffaloes can also be seen here, but they are the exception rather than the rule.

So many of the earth's wild areas are in danger of being lost and yet somehow, as you fly over or look out across this huge expanse of wilderness, you perceive a ray of hope for the future. Admittedly, inhospitable areas are not very desirable to man and the Makgadikgadi may be one of those areas, but only time will tell whether or not 'civilised' man will despoil this environment as he has so many others.

It may be appropriate to state here that Botswana has set

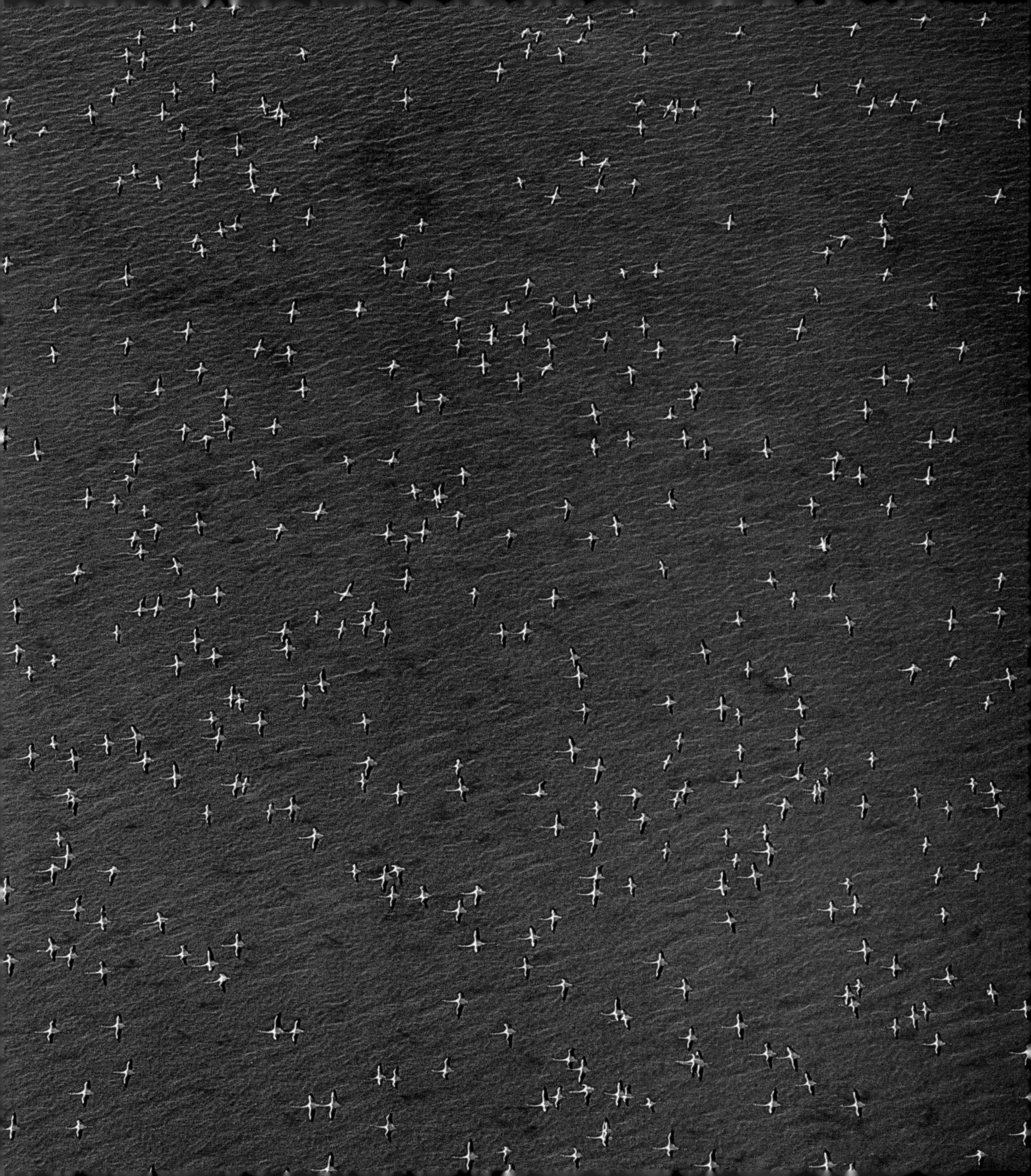

Hoof-marks in the sun-baked crust of Ntwetwe Pan are evidence of the recent passing of a small herd of antelope or zebra in search of water or fresh grazing.

aside over 101 000 km² – more than 17 per cent of its total land surface – for national parks and nature reserves, and it needs support and encouragement to maintain these areas for all time.

The birdlife of Makgadikgadi is worth mentioning, and an excellent checklist has already been compiled. Of particular interest are the large raptors which in Makgadikgadi are not threatened as their relatives in other parts of southern Africa

are. Flocks of waterbirds, including flamingoes and pelicans, inhabit the pans during the summer rainfall period from December to April.

A special attraction at Kudiakam, a pan south of Nxai Pan, are the Baines' Baobabs, which the artist Thomas Baines painted in May 1862 when he outspanned here and set up his easel. These baobabs, at the edge of the pan, are also known as the 'Sleeping Sisters' and the 'Seven Sisters'.

A group of Burchell's zebra and a pair of blue wildebeest kick up salt-laden dust from a small pan in the Makgadikgadi Pans Game Reserve. Beyond the pan, ostriches are dwarfed by the immensity of the sea of grass extending to the far horizon.

There can be few harsher environments than that of the Makgadikgadi Pans. Periodic flooding as in Sowa Pan (above) allows aquatic plant and animal life to flourish, but in salinities at levels which would be toxic to 'ordinary' freshwater organisms. As the pans evaporate (right), searing heat and year-long drought require that these various forms of life develop desiccation-resistant resting-stages in the form of spores, eggs or underground cocoons which lie dormant until the next inundation.

CHAPTER SIX

CHOBE NATIONAL PARK AND SAVUTI

Chobe National Park covers an area of 11 646 km² in the northern part of Botswana. The park and its adjacent areas, which have such an intimate link with the Okavango Delta, are generally flat, but there is undulating countryside and altitudes range from 930 m in the south-west to 1 000 m above sea level in the north-east.

This generally featureless terrain conta ns yet another relic lake bed in the south-west known as the Mababe Depression. In former times, the lake was fed from the north by the Kwando River which flowed into the Linyanti Swamp and out through the Savuti Channel and Marsh to Mababe. The southern end of the Mababe was fed by the Khwai River from the Okavango Delta. North and east of Mababe, there is a low-lying escarpment; in the west, a sand ridge known as Magwikhwe, which runs parallel to the Savuti Marsh. Another ridge running parallel and adjacent to the Chobe River in the north extends all the way through to Kasane at the north-east corner of Botswana. There are hills in the south of the Park at Chinamba and at Gcoha and Gubatsha in the vicinity of the Savuti Marsh.

The park's drainage system is influenced by the Okavango and Chobe rivers, which originate in the Angolan highlands, and by the Zambezi River, which rises in western Zambia. The Chobe, or Kwando, as it is known in its upper reaches, flows through the Caprivi which is administered by South West Africa/Namibia and forms the southern boundary of the vast wetland system known as the Linyanti Swamp. Here the river changes its name to the Linyanti. Further east, at Ngoma, it becomes the Chobe.

The Zambezi River forms the boundary between Zambia and the Caprivi, and at Kazungula, Botswana, South West Africa/Namibia, Zambia and Zimbabwe have a common meeting point in the river. From here, the mighty Zambezi carries the eastward flow of water over the Victoria Falls, being the only seaward release of any water that may have originated in the Okavango River. Such water would leave the Okavango at the base of the panhandle around Seronga and flow along the Selinda (or Magwegqana) Spillway. The water overflow down the spillway is sporadic, however, and it has not flowed for many years. When it does flow, it is fed into the Linyanti Swamp.

Flowing southwards out of the Linyanti Swamp via Zibadianja Lagoon is the Savuti Channel. When seen by David

A herd of elephants wades across the upper Savuti Channel close to the Zibadianja Lagoon at the southern tip of the Linyanti Swamp.

Fresh from his afternoon mud-bath, a bull elephant stands beneath a dead camel-thorn tree in the Savuti Channel near Savuti Marsh. The channel's flow is capricious and unpredictable and over its recorded history of 130 years has flowed and dried up alternately on several occasions. It stopped flowing in 1982, and, at the time of writing, is still empty of water.

Livingstone in 1853, it contained water; Frederick Courteney Selous, the big-game hunter, observed it in 1879 and by then it was dry; in 1923 the hunter A. G. Stigand also saw that it was dry. The water of the channel began flowing again in 1957, but had dried up again by 1966. It flowed again from April 1967 until 1982 when it started drying up again. It still remains dry. The reasons why this mysterious channel has switched on and off during the last 114 years have never been fully accounted for, although tectonic rather than hydrological factors seem to be the most plausible.

Prior to 1957, during the long (perhaps 70-year) period the Savuti Channel was dry, large camel-thorns (*Acacia erioloba*), were able to grow in its sandy bed. They died when the channel started flowing. Camel-thorn trees, however, are abundant in this beautiful area of Chobe National Park.

Finally, mention must be made of the Linyanti Swamp which extends southwards on the east side of the Kwando River, past Zibadianja Lagoon and then follows a line northeastwards to the Chobe River. The swamp is between two and 30 km wide, and the area is dominated by phragmites reed and papyrus. Much of the mainstream is blocked by reeds. The broad floodplains consist mainly of open grass-

A family group of elephants passes through the fresh green growth of mopane after the onset of the summer rains in the Savuti Marsh area of Chobe National Park. Although elephants eat a wide range of plant species, mopane is a particularly favoured food.

After crossing the upper Savuti Channel, a herd of elephants makes its way eastwards along its sandy banks. The elephant population of northern Botswana, presently estimated at around 40 000, is expanding beyond the environment's capacity to support it. Research is currently being undertaken to calculate the optimum population size and to assess various methods of reducing their numbers.

land, interspersed with large termite-mounds which are colonised by various trees. The swamp is home to a variety of animals. However, poaching continues to cause concern for the survival of the area's larger forms of wildlife, in particular lechwe, hippos, giraffes and, to some extent, elephants on the Caprivi side.

Along the Botswanan bank of the Linyanti one finds one of the least-known and most spectacular wild areas in Botswana. This vast area of the Chobe National Park, with the exception of Kachikau in the north, is devoid of permanent human habitation. Kachikau is the home of the Basubiya

people who settled here around the turn of the century. There is no swamp on the Botswanan side of the Chobe River between Ngoma and Kasane, although there are small floodplains which are seasonally inundated. The more extensive floodplains on the opposite bank in Caprivi are inhabited by people farming with livestock.

This then describes rather sketchily the north-eastern area of our journey which has followed the waters of the Okavango. For most of the journey, our home base was the Savuti Marsh – one of the finest game-viewing areas in Botswana. Famous for its bull elephants and lions, the marsh

covers an area of 80 km² and is dominated by couch- or kweek grass (*Cynodon dactylon*). The road to Maun skirts the western side, with the Magwikhwe sand ridge running roughly parallel to the marsh.

Our hosts at Savuti were Lloyd and June Wilmot who, with their son Ashley and their loyal staff, manage Lloyd's Camp. The camp, lying on the south side of the Savuti Channel, is one of three private camps located in this part of the park. There is also a public camp-site for those who prefer to be more independent.

Prior to 1982, the winding channel carried a gently flow-

ing, crystal-clear stream of water which emptied into the Savuti Marsh. At that time groups of hippos and crocodiles were abundant and fish life was plentiful; if you sat on the banks of the Savuti Channel you could easily see herds of game, including buffaloes and elephants. When the marsh began drying up, the huge concentration of game was forced to disperse.

In spite of the dispersion of the game, all the large predators still occur here, including lions, leopards, cheetahs, wild dogs and spotted hyaenas. If you are lucky, you will even see a lion kill. There are also numerous giraffes, baboons

A lone bull elephant walks away from the water-hole in front of Lloyd's Camp on the south bank of the Savuti Channel near Savuti Marsh. No water has flowed along this section of the channel since 1982 but artificial watering-points have been constructed to provide for the requirements of a continuous stream of elephant and other game animals.

Previous page: An elephant indulges in a dust-bath in the dry mopane woodland between Savuti Marsh and the Linyanti Swamp. Dust- or mud-baths help to ward off the sun's rays and the attentions of irritating insects.

Left: Trees cast late-afternoon shadows over the yellowed grasses of the northern section of Savuti Marsh in Chobe National Park. The Gubatsha and Qango hills relieve an otherwise monotonously flat landscape. The presence or absence of water in the marsh varies with the seasons and with the amount of water fed into it via the Savuti Channel. When water is present, the region plays host to one of the greatest wildlife concentrations in Africa.

Below: High-stepping ostriches trot through soft grey sand in the mopane woodland in the south-west corner of Chobe National Park adjacent to Moremi Wildlife Reserve. When pressed by predators, these large and powerful birds can achieve speeds of up to 65 kilometres per hour. If cornered, however, they can defend themselves very adequately by delivering damaging kicks with their uniquely two-toed feet.

and troops of vervet monkeys, and the birdlife is prolific.

Between March and April, when the pans are still full of water, thousands of zebras migrate through Savuti Marsh on their way north, sometimes accompanied by tsessebe and blue wildebeest. Buffalo, however, are not as plentiful as they used to be, many of the old bulls having been pulled down by the marsh's several prides of lions. Roan and sable antelope may be seen at the water-hole near the public camp mentioned earlier.

Although lions are said to be the main attraction at Savuti, for me the elephants take pride of place. Nowhere in my travels have I encountered bull elephants that are so tolerant of humans, or that will be so calm when you approach them. In 1982, when Iain and Oria Douglas-Hamilton, the well-known authors of *Among the Elephants*, paid a visit to Savuti, Oria sat for hours on a pile of old elephant dung at Harvey's Pan watching various groups of bull elephants splashing about and drinking during the noonday heat, completely indifferent to her presence. After dinner that evening at Lloyd's Camp, 'Baby Huey', a large bull elephant, blundered over the tent guy-ropes, stopped a short distance away from our group sitting around the fire, and peered down at us for fully two minutes. He then sauntered off between the kitchen and a row of tents towards the river.

These elephants are placid compared with those in areas where they are disturbed by humans and firearms. Well-meaning but misinformed tourists who feed elephants are unwittingly contributing to a major problem — the pachyderms often become violent in their quest for hand-fed delicacies such as fruit. A famous elephant named Elroy had to be shot for this reason and, while this book was being written, the same fate has overtaken Huey.

Honey-badgers, like the elephants of Savuti, have little fear of man and they often visit the camps in the Chobe National Park, wandering in and out of the tents during their nightly foraging. Hyaenas, too, are never far away, and tourists have learnt the hard way that leaving their leather bush-shoes outside their tents is a mistake, as they are certain to be gone the next morning.

The orchestrated calls of hyaenas, jackals and lions across

the dry sandveld of Savuti leave exciting memories of this very special place.

Man has lived in Savuti a long, long time. This fact was confirmed in 1969 when Tim Liversedge, who lives in Maun and is very familiar with northern Botswana, discovered rock paintings on the Gubatsha Hills overlooking the Savuti Marsh. One of the five sites lies quite close to the dry channel, and is some 10 m above the ground. It features a lovely painting of an elephant, sable, giraffe and eland in red ochre on a smooth rock slab. This evidence of early settlement at Gubatsha Hills is most interesting, being so far from the nearest known sites of rock paintings at the Tsodilo Hills, across the Okavango Delta in the west.

One mammal species you are not likely to see in Savuti is the black rhino (*Diceros bicornis*), whose numbers have declined to fewer than 4 000 throughout the African continent. According to Peter Hitchins, noted black rhinoceros specialist, there are three recognised subspecies of black rhino in southern Africa. We are familiar with two of them, namely *D. bicornis minor*, found in Zululand, the Kruger National Park and Zimbabwe, and *D. bicornis bicornis*, found in South West Africa/Namibia and now in the Augrabies Falls and Vaalbos national parks to which they were translocated from Etosha in 1985 and 1987. Included in this latter subspecies are the famous desert rhinos of the Kaokoveld which have received considerable attention in the last few years.

But what about the third subspecies, *D. bicornis chobiensis*, from northern Botswana and south-east Angola? Many believe it to be extinct, yet sightings of black rhinoceros have been recorded in this region during the past few decades. A professional hunter, Darryl Dandridge, saw a black rhino in the Kwando area near the Linyanti Swamp some years ago, and more recently the biologist Petri Viljoen spotted a large male black rhino at the southern end of Savuti Marsh whilst radio-tracking from an aircraft. Several other independent sightings of spoor have also been noted.

Reports indicate that the most likely area in which the subspecies *may* still occur is the Kwando-Linyanti region, which falls within a controlled hunting area. As discussed earlier, the Kwando River flows between the eastern Caprivi and northern Botswana and drains into the Linyanti Swamp. The water spreads out over a large area, mainly in Caprivi. This area is characterised by vast, open grassland, phragmites-reed and papyrus swamp. The regions to the south and west are covered with dry thornveld, mopane woodland and Kalahari sand. Camel-thorn and *Burkea* (wild seringa) woodland dominate the edges of the Linyanti Swamp. No-one lives there permanently and it is not easily accessible to the tourist.

A herd of buffalo mills about under the leafless winter canopy of wild syringa (*Burkea africana*) woodland between the Linyanti Swamp and Savuti Marsh. Buffalo are very sensitive to heat and in hot weather tend to seek shade by day and feed by night.

Left: With manes tossing and black tails flying in the wind, a group of blue wildebeest gallops across the lush green summer sward of the Savuti Marsh. Although it has received no water from the Savuti Channel since 1982, summer rains are sufficient to rejuvenate the vegetation and to allow pools of water to form, making this part of the Mababe Depression a magnet for a splendid array of large mammals.

Below: The graceful impala is one of the most common of Savuti's antelope species. It favours lightly wooded habitats and feeds on grass as well as on the fine twigs and leaves of a variety of trees and shrubs. When fleeing from predators it is capable of enormous bounds of up to twelve metres, an accomplishment which is enough to disconcert even the most determined of lions.

In his book, *A Hunter's Wanderings in Africa*, Selous observed that in 1879 there were still two or three black rhinos along the upper Chobe, north-west of the Sunta outlet. However, he added that there were none between the Chobe and the Zambezi Rivers, and that there never had been any there.

In 1968, in a detailed ecological report to the Food and Agriculture Organisation of the United Nations, Graham Child, a former Director of Wildlife in Botswana, noted various sightings between 1963 and 1967 in and around the Chobe National Park area, including the Gcoha and Gubatsha hills, Ngoma, the region traversed by the Linyanti and Kwando Rivers, and the Magwikhwe ridge south of Savuti. The late Bobby Wilmot and his hunters also reported seeing these rhinos in the Okavango and on Chief's Island.

Although the late Dr. Reay Smithers, author of *The Mammals of the Southern African Subregion*, suggested that the black rhinoceros probably disappeared in Botswana by about 1974, the reports by Dandridge and Viljoen indicated that it did still exist in the wilder areas of eastern Caprivi and

northern Botswana. Some years ago, Peter Hitchins brought up the subject of *chobiensis* and felt that something should be done to establish the facts.

I started asking questions, but drew a blank. Very few people, other than Viljoen and Dandridge, had seen a black rhino in recent times. Hitchins wanted to get into the region and talk to the local inhabitants.

'The rhinos must be there,' he kept saying, but nobody seemed too interested, mostly because of the remoteness of the region and its inaccessibility. He asked me to investigate the rhinoceros depicted in the Bushman paintings at the Tsodilo Hills; we did this with Lloyd Wilmot as our guide and found that they were indeed black rhinos.

Later, when Herman Potgieter and I were gathering material for this book, André, my son Anton and I went directly to Guma Lagoon where we planned to spend the night; Lloyd and Herman followed at first light in Lloyd's Cessna 175 to film the lower part of the Okavango Delta. West of Savuti, there is a large pan in the middle of a vast, dry area.

Known as Tsantsara, this pan used to be part of one of the drainage rivers which carried water from the Linyanti via Zibadianja Lagoon to the Mababe Depression and it is the only water to be found in this immense wilderness at certain times of the year. Some years ago. I loyd discovered the carcass of a large white rhinoceros which had become bogged down in the thick mud of the pan.

On this occasion, on their way to the Okavango, Lloyd and Herman flew low in a wide circle towards the pan, which as the crow flies is 30 km from Linyanti, and there she was — a female black rhinoceros and her calf. Lloyd made a number of passes as she ran off into the dry *Terminalia* woodland. Was this actually a specimen of *chobiensis*? And with a strapping big calf? Imagine our excitement when we heard the news later on.

Herman's photographs later confirmed that it was, indeed, a black rhinoceros, and we reported this to John Benn, the Chief Game Warden of Ngamiland. A nature conservation officer based in Caprivi later confirmed that a few still occur in western Caprivi.

The continued existence of black rhinos in this area of Botswana is good news indeed, and whether or not they are in fact of the subspecies *chobiensis* does not matter. What is important is the black rhino's survival and its future in Botswana, and with the overall decline of the species in Africa, its presence in northern Ngamiland is encouraging.

Flying up the dry Savuti Channel one October afternoon, we see small family groups of elephants in dry woodland, a herd of 20 sable standing idly in the shade and, above and below us, marabou storks soaring gracefully, their legs straight and their necks tucked in characteristically. These

Above: Tails characteristically erect, two warthog run from the noise of our approaching aircraft, one nimbly hurdling a fallen tree.
Left: One of Africa's most endangered mammal species, the black rhinoceros, photographed near Tsantsara Pan just inside the western boundary of Chobe National Park. In recent years, poaching has reached catastrophic proportions and fewer than 3 700 black rhino are now believed to survive in the whole of Africa. Our confirmation of the survival of a breeding group of rhinoceros in this remote part of Botswana is most encouraging.

Below: South of Savuti Marsh in the southern section of Chobe National Park is the Mababe Depression, a huge flat expanse of grassland with occasional clumps of scattered bush. Like the Makgadikgadi Pans, Mababe is a 'fossil' lake-bed relic of the ancient Kalahari 'super-lake' and, when it has been blessed with good rains, its fertile soil provides rich grazing for multitudes of large herbivores, from zebra, giraffe and elephant to impala, red hartebeest, tsessebe and blue wildebeest – and rich pickings for large carnivores such as lion, cheetah, spotted hyaena and hunting dog.

Right: Surprised near a Mababe water-hole, a Burchell's zebra bolts to safety. The Mababe Depression forms part of the northern Ngamiland zebra migration route.

scavengers may appear macabre on the ground, but are marvellous to watch in the air. The storks peer at us with disdain, banking away at our noisy approach. We rush past them, thankful that we have never hit one. They are large birds, 1,3 m tall, and are capable of soaring to great heights.

The channel starts to twist and turn as we approach the Linyanti Swamp, and pools of water become more frequent. Grazing is virtually non-existent and the summer rains have not yet started. Hot air rises continuously, buffeting the aircraft. Fish-eagles are lined up on a narrow channel below us, awaiting their chance to drag out a trapped barbel in a muddy pool; saddle-billed storks stand in the shallows as pied kingfishers hover overhead; lechwe stand or lie on the dry ground as warthogs scurry to and fro. We see more elephants in the bush and along the edges of the channels and lagoons. Water is now abundant, but not so the grass.

Now we can see some 500 to 600 buffalo, moving in a slow, dusty line towards water. There are so many of them that they look like black ants.

Hippos are in every stretch of water, but the stench of decaying flesh which rises up 70 m to our aircraft confirms that many of them are dead. We count dozens of lifeless forms in the water and on the ground. For them, the rains have come too late and they now lie bloated and rotting. For once nature is the cause, not man, and the toll inflicted is a sobering reminder of the ravages of drought.

We pass over the Zibadianja Lagoon and turn right, following the waters of the Linyanti River downstream. To our left, the vast floodplains stretch out endlessly, and a huge column of smoke rises from a grass fire in Caprivi. We hug the Botswana side of the Linyanti River, with its thick stands of acacia trees. Further over to our right, the dry thornveld stretches out to distant horizons. We are careful not to fly into the Caprivi, for it is difficult to determine the border.

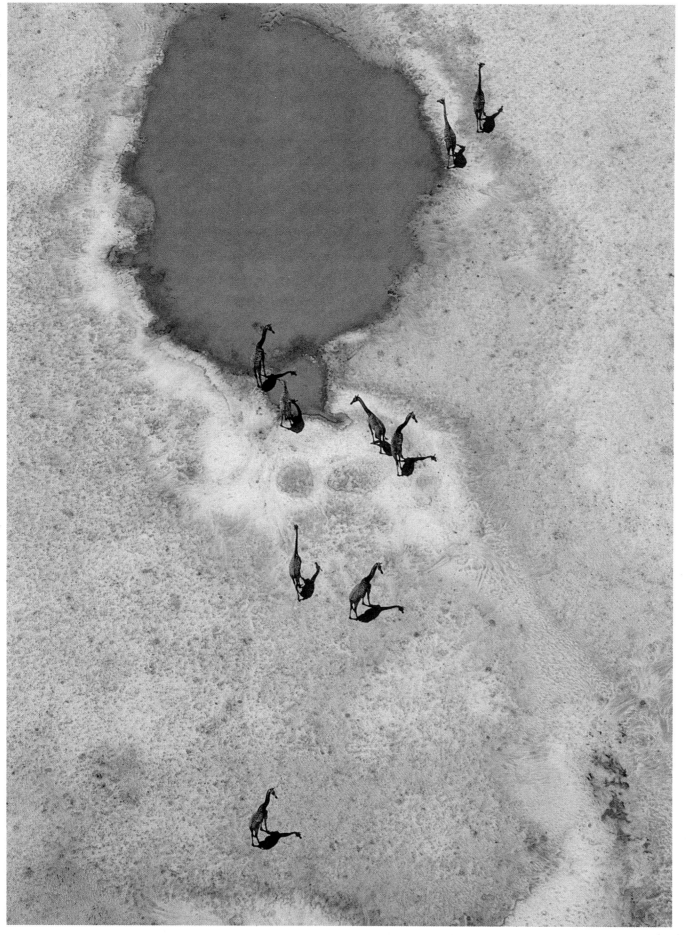

Left: A group of giraffe stalks warily to drink at Harvey's Pan near Savuti in the middle of the dry season. When drinking, they adopt an awkward stance with their forelegs splayed widely apart and are vulnerable to predation. Giraffe will drink if water is available but, like many herbivores of semi-arid savanna country, if necessary can obtain all their moisture requirements from their food-plants.

Above: These three giraffe in the woodland between Savuti Marsh and the Linyanti River just outside the Chobe National Park seem unable to pinpoint the direction from which our aircraft is approaching. The giraffe's only serious predator is the lion, but although they are successfully hunted on occasion, sometimes the tables are turned and a well-placed giraffe kick has been known to kill the king of beasts.

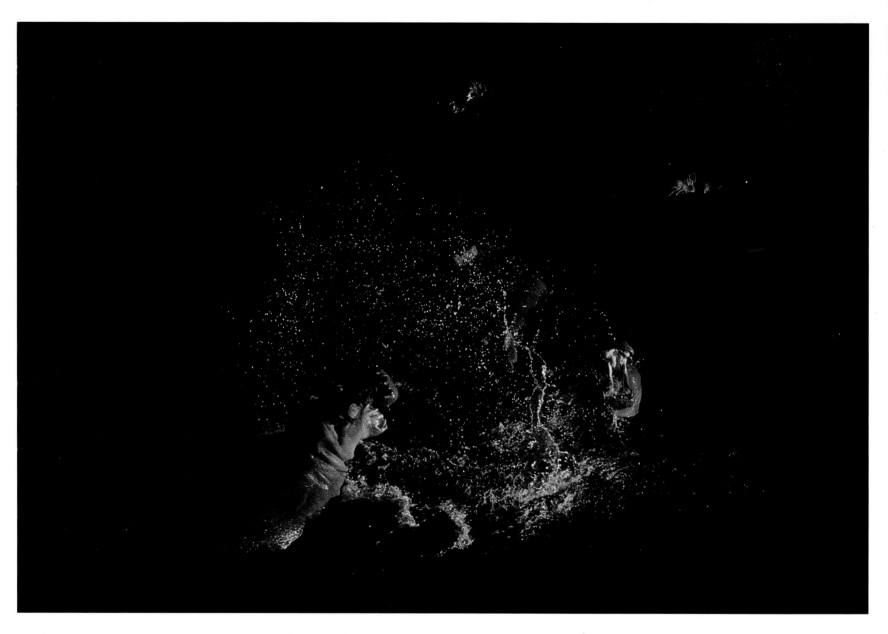

In a flurry of water two hippopotamus bulls challenge each other for supremacy in the Linyanti River. Their tusk-like canine teeth are capable of causing severe injury, and death frequently results from such territorial battles.

Passing over the beautiful Linyanti Camp on the banks of the Linyanti River, we see buffaloes standing belly-deep in water, cattle-egrets in attendance. Every now and then, the water opens up into a lagoon surrounded by reeds varying in colour through a range of greens and yellows. Turning to port we see four bull elephants heading speedily across the firm floodplain towards Botswana. Turning around again, we see a large crocodile basking in the sun and a group of white-backed vultures standing at the edge of the water with outspread wings. We turn around once more and head for northern Chobe, and the famed Chobe Game Lodge overlooking the Chobe River.

This superbly situated lodge is one of several establishments which attract tourists and wildlife enthusiasts visiting the Chobe National Park. Another is Chobe Chilwero, run by Brian and Jan Graham, just outside the park's entrance. To return to the cool comfort of one of these lodges after a hot, dusty, exciting day adds greatly to the pleasure of one's African experience.

The Chobe Safari Lodge, situated at Kasane, a short distance from the park, offers comfortable accommodation and a camping ground adjacent to the lodge. Then there is Kubu Lodge, some 10 km from Kasane on the road to Kazungula.

Kasane is the administrative headquarters for the Chobe district, and it is said that no one lives there permanently — they only go there to find work. The town has a health centre, police post, a few general stores and is the headquarters for some hunting and photographic safari companies. It is one of those African towns that developed out of necessity rather than with any thought of design, and it has its share of pollution brought about by its growing population. Because of this, it could pose a challenge for the environmentally conscious — being so close to one of Africa's most beautiful national parks.

The northern part of Chobe National Park is famous for its large concentrations of elephant, but research over the years indicates that the park cannot support so many of these animals. Of the estimated 40 000 or more elephants in northern

Before the Savuti Channel ceased flowing in 1982, hippopotamus could be encountered all along its 60-kilometre length from the Linyanti Swamp to the Savuti Marsh. Many hundreds died when the channel dried up. This school dispersing hurriedly to the safety of deep water was photographed in the 'Garden of Eden' area of the Savuti Channel near its exit from the Linyanti River. The dead trees are leadwoods (*Combretum imberbe*) which flourished in one of the channel's previous dry phrases but which died in 1957 when water started to flow again after decades of drought.

139

Left: The Linyanti River forms part of the boundary between Botswana and the eastern section of the Caprivi Strip of South West Africa/Namibia. The Linyanti Swamp on the Caprivi side of the river teems with wildlife and is home to buffalo, elephant, sitatunga, hippopotamus, lechwe and crocodile amongst many others. The grass- and marshland on the left is in the Caprivi Strip; the wooded area interspersed with water-filled pans on the right is part of the Chobe National Park.

Above: Waterbuck disturbed from a late-afternoon siesta on the banks of the Savuti Channel rise to their feet and run off, the characteristic white 'targets' around their rumps prominently displayed.

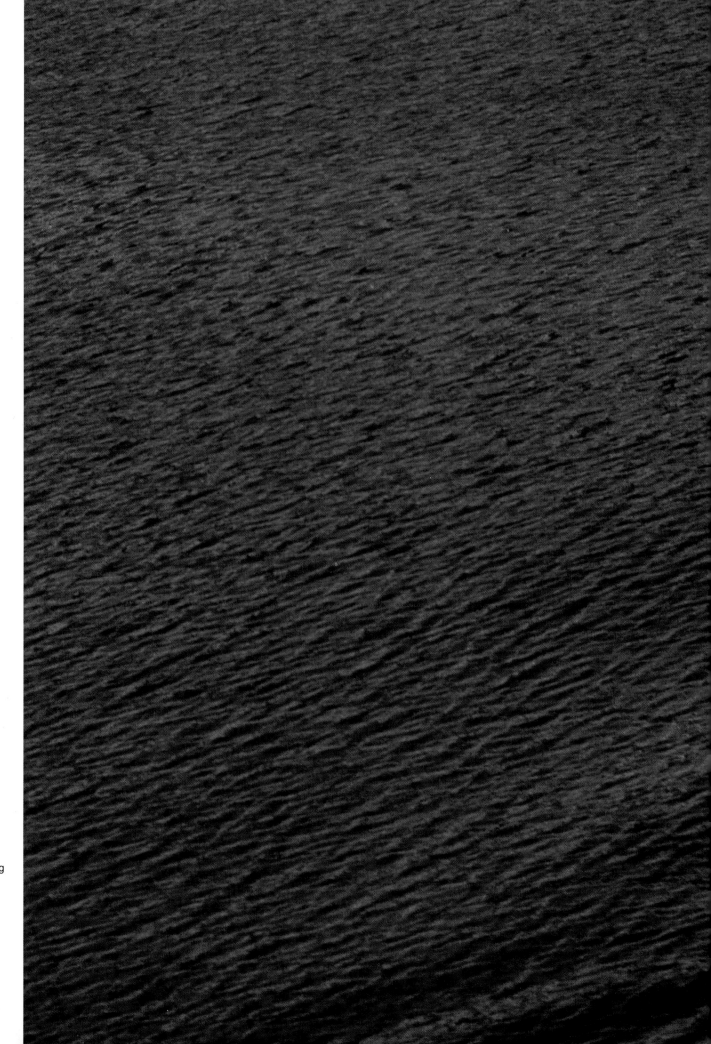

A bull elephant emigrates from the Caprivi Strip to Botswana by walking and swimming across the Linyanti River. Elephants are common on both sides of the rather ill-defined international boundary in the Linyanti Swamp and pay no attention to man's geopolitical manipulations.

142

Botswana, about 8 000 occur along the Chobe River, between Ngoma and Kasane. In 1874 Selous encountered relatively few in this area — a good indication of how they have proliferated in their migration into Botswana from the Zimbabwe border. Evidence of their large numbers is quite apparent from the destruction to the woodland of the region — particularly to the camel-thorn and knob-thorn trees. At the height of the dry season, large numbers of elephant congregate along the Chobe River as the pans in the south dry out; during the wet season, there are concentrations in the Ngwezumba area, 40-50 km south of the Chobe River.

Interestingly enough, although elephants were found at Lake Ngami as far back as 1870, they had disappeared by the turn of the century. A major survey is currently being undertaken by George Calef, a biologist employed by the Department of Wildlife and National Parks, to ascertain the status and movement of northern Botswana's elephants. Using a helicopter, George has marked about 50 with radio collars to plot their movements. It is hoped that his project will provide the basis for a management plan which will ensure the long-term survival of Botswana's elephants. Botswana is very fortunate in having such large areas where elephants can roam, but the decision may have to be made sooner or later whether or not to reduce their numbers.

Poachers from Caprivi have been killing unsuspecting elephants from their dugouts at night — and surveillance in the

Richly caparisoned in sable and argent, a squadron of zebras stands idle among the trampled golden grass of the Linyanti floodplain in the late dry season.

Above: The waters of the Linyanti Swamp flow north-eastwards for over 100 kilometres through a broad floodplain with a shifting main river channel. As the river separates the Caprivi Strip of South West Africa/Namibia from Botswana, the international border between the two countries cannot be clearly determined in this area.

Left: Palm-trees and a handful of people – but little else – flourish on the dry sandy ridge near Parakurungu south of Lake Liambezi on the Linyanti floodplain.

Above: What was the Kwando, then the Linyanti, is now the Chobe River as it sweeps past the beautifully sited Chobe Game Lodge twelve kilometres from Kasane in the north-east corner of Botswana. This well-appointed and popular lodge is an enclave of affluence and opulence in the heart of unspoiled Africa.
Right: Near Kasane the Chobe River has a clearly defined channel but its floodplain is marshland interwoven with backwaters, oxbow lakes and numerous pools.

area has been stepped up in an effort to halt the senseless slaughter. Victims also include white rhinos introduced from Zululand.

It is a fantastic sight to observe the elephant along the narrow edge of the flood plain on the Botswana side from the decks of the *Mosi-oa-Tunya,* the beautiful boat that once plied the waters of the great Zambezi River above the Victoria Falls in Zimbabwe (and now based at the Chobe Game Lodge), or to take your own small craft and slowly pilot your way upstream and quietly watch the variety of animal life that frequents the river. Apart from elephants, several other large mammal species use the Chobe River. They include puku which, although more common in eastern Caprivi, also inhabit the Botswanan side of the floodplain known as the Pookoo Flats. The handsome males, weighing around 70 kg,

are often seen alone or in small family groups. They are always found near water, preferring open grassland bordering on swamps, vleis and rivers. They are sometimes mistaken for lechwe, but their horns are shorter and they don't have black markings on the legs as lechwe do.

Another resident of the Chobe River's hinterland is the 'Chobe' bushbuck (*Tragelaphus scriptus ornatus*), a subspecies which has more distinctive markings than bushbuck found elsewhere. Buffaloes and hippos are abundant in the area, as are giraffes, impala and kudu. Waterbuck may be found mingling with the lechwe and puku along the narrow floodplain. The large predators are here too, but are not seen as often as they are in Savuti.

You can't visit Chobe and not notice the birdlife which abounds along the river's floodplain and inland bush. If you

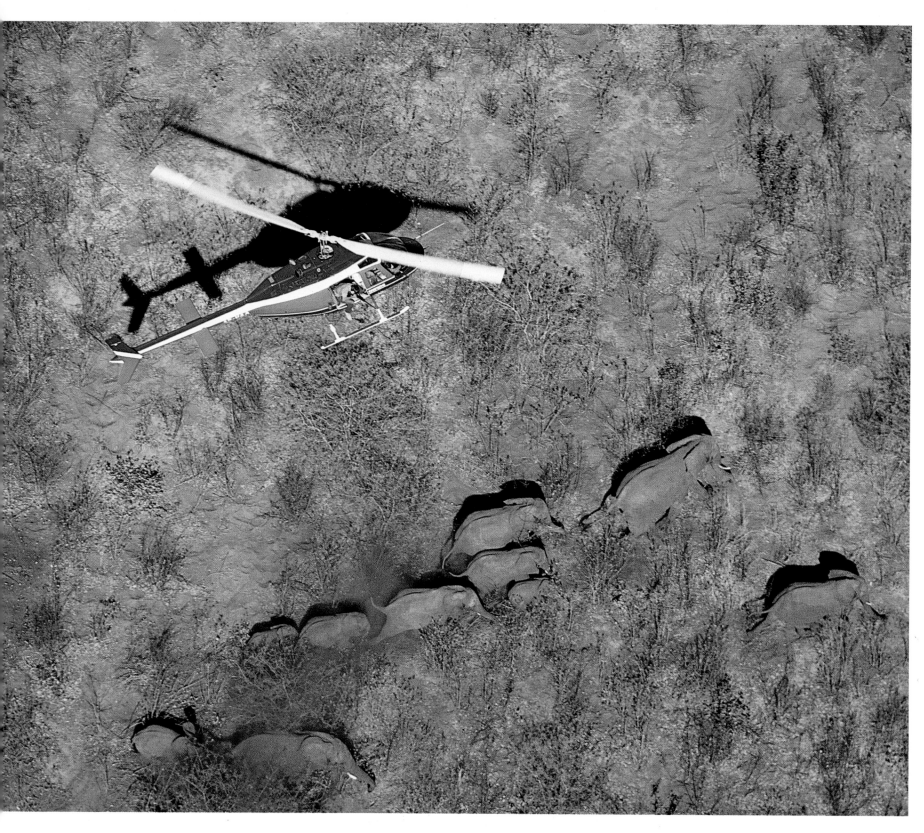

Far left: Thanks to the remoteness of Chobe National Park, Botswana's elephant population has increased dramatically over the last few decades. Estimates put their numbers at around 40 000 – thought to be more than their environment can safely support. Research is therefore being conducted into their movements and population densities, in part by tranquillising selected elephants and fitting them with radio-collars. Here biologist George Calef takes aim at his chosen target in Chobe National Park south-east of Kasane.
Left: George Calef (kneeling) and Fred Mitchell prepare to attach a radio-collar to an unconscious elephant. Fifty elephants have been fitted with such radio-collars under this research programme and their movements are regularly monitored and plotted.

Buffalo, not cattle, graze peacefully on a floodplain island in the Chobe River between Kasane and Chobe Game Lodge.

sit quietly in the grounds of one of the lodges or cruise up the river you will most likely see Egyptian and spurwinged geese, blacksmith plovers, black-winged stilts, grey-headed gulls, rock pratincoles, three-banded plovers, greenshanks, hamerkops, little stints, ruffs and marsh sandpipers.

As dawn breaks, the river takes on various shades of pink; there is a pervading tranquillity, and you feel completely at one with nature. It is clear that people come here not only for the wildlife, but to experience this unity with the real Africa of old. If you consider that the world's natural environment is diminishing daily, the price one pays to visit this beautiful place is not excessive. Who, after all, can ever put a price on the scenes described here?

Lesser striped swallows sit on the wall outside with their distinctive *eh-eh-eh-eh* call-notes. A baboon is barking in the bush, and across the river two fishermen in a dugout are setting out their nets. A Caprivi resident is walking two oxen towards a distant row of reed huts. Down below me at the water's edge a flock of guinea-fowl scratch about in the dust. Lechwe are out on the floodplain, and the waters of the Chobe River are as flat as a mirror. A fish-eagle calls from a distant perch as white-breasted cormorants head upstream on frantically beating wings to a destination only they know. A pied kingfisher hovers, then dives rapidly, entering the water with beak forward and wings pinned back. It emerges awkwardly on short wings and flits off to perch on a dead

Oxpeckers in attendance, this school of hippopotamus prepares to return to the water after a mid-morning sunbathing session on the banks of the Chobe River upstream of Kasane.

Below: Although clumsy on land – and perhaps a little top-heavy with its massive bill and capacious yellow throat-poach – the white pelican is an accomplished and powerful flier. It typically flies in V-formation and on migration can travel between 400 and 500 kilometres per day. It is more commonly seen on the Chobe River floodplain than its relative the pink-backed pelican.

Right: With its long legs trailing behind, a goliath heron cocks a wary eye over its shoulder as it flies in unwilling tandem with our Cessna 175 over the Chobe River floodplain.

tree in the water. An African jacana pokes its beak between the water-lilies growing along the edge; then it leaps on to another leaf as it begins to sink. Hippos call across the floodplain as the light starts changing from the mauves and pinks of dawn to the brighter light of morning. To the east, the sun pushes its head over a baobab-covered ridge that runs parallel to the Chobe River.

From here, the river wends its way towards Zimbabwe be-

fore merging with the mighty Zambezi River to carry the waters of our story towards and over the spectacular Victoria Falls – *Mosi-oa-Tunya* or 'The Smoke That Thunders' – onwards through Zimbabwe to Mozambique and, finally, into the Indian Ocean.

An old and dry land, the nation of Botswana has one treasure she must guard and protect for it is the only one of its kind – the Okavango.

The mighty Zambezi crashes over the Victoria Falls on its way eastwards to the Indian Ocean. Even in the dry season it carries sufficient water to create the billowing clouds of mist and spray that give the falls their Kalolo-Lozi name – *Mosi-oa-Tunya* or 'The Smoke That Thunders'. In very wet years, when the Angolan floodwaters are particularly high, some of the Okavango's water overflows into the Magwegqana (Selinda) Spillway near Seronga and trickles eastwards to the Kwando/Linyanti system; from the Linyanti it flows to the Chobe, from the Chobe it flows to the Zambezi, and thus eventually adds its small splash to the magnificent Victoria Falls.